Poets, like painters, thus unskill'd to trace
The naked nature and the living grace,
With gold and jewels cover every part,
And hide with ornaments their want of art.
Alexander Pope
Essay on Criticism

For I will for no man's pleasure
Pedants shall not tie my strains
To our antique poets' veins;
Being born as free as these,
I will sing as I shall please.
George Wither
The Shepherd's Hunting

Aut insanit aut versus facit.
(The man is mad, or else he's writing verses.)
Horace
Satires

Poets utter great and wise things which they do not themselves understand.
Plato
The Republic

Painting is silent poetry, and poetry is painting with the gift of speech.
Plutarch
De Gloria Atheniensium

What has reasoning to do with the art of painting? … To generalise is to be an
idiot.
William Blake
from Gilchrist's *Life*

Go, litel bok, go, litel myn tragedye,
Ther God thi makere yet, er that he dye,
So sende myght to make in som comedye!
But litel book, no makyng thow n'envie,
But subgit be to alle poesye;
And kis the steppes, where as thow seest pace
Virgile, Ovide, Omer, Lucan and Stace.
Geoffrey Chaucer
Troilus and Criseyde

Painted into a Corner

Faysal Mikdadi

- Lulu.com -

First published in 2014

Printed and distributed through www.lulu.com

Cover design and Author's photograph by Faysal Mikdadi

Paintings so ascribed are by the author 2003-2013

The poet sketched by an unknown artist in a café in Royal Wootton Bassett. Gifted to the poet in the late 1990s.

Faysal Mikdadi, born in Palestine in 1948, was carried to Lebanon where he was brought up and given his rather unsuccessful education. He moved to Britain in 1967 and has lived there since. He is an English Literature specialist with a keen interest in the Nineteenth Century

Victorian novel and in Shakespeare. His published works include novels, poems, short stories, bibliographies, educational essays and regular contributions on current affairs.

He started writing at a very early age during a turbulent and unhappy childhood. His urge to write comes from a deeply felt need to try to make sense of a disordered and crazy world and to laugh at his own rather stodgy attitudes to a much sought after quiet life. It also comes from his need to laugh at others' predictable higgledy piggledy existence and to celebrate his deep love of nature – the only place in which he sees any order and a semblance of logic.

These poems were composed at various times over the years. They, and the few paintings by the author, included, were the poet's attempts to make some sense out of the incomprehensible.

By the Same Author

Novels:

Chateaux en Palestine, Paris, France, 1982.

Tamra, London, United Kingdom, 1988.

Return, Raleigh NC, USA, 2008.

Snowflake, Raleigh NC, USA, 2013.

Short Stories:

Christmas Stories, Raleigh NC, USA, 2012.

The Dabawis and the Shargawis, Raleigh NC, USA, 2013.

Poetry:

A Return: The Siege of Beirut, London, United Kingdom, 1983.

Bibliographies:

Gamal Abdel Nasser, Westport, USA, 1991.

Margaret Thatcher, Westport, USA, 1993.

These poems and paintings are dedicated to my wife Susan and to my

children Catherine and Richard. Thank you for your kind support.

Contents

Illustrations

Each illustration's or picture's name or description is followed first by its source and then by the title of the poem which it accompanies. Every effort has been made to identify the correct source of each illustration or picture. If an error is spotted, please get in touch with the poet on fhm481812@aol.com and the error will be immediately amended.

The illustration preceding the brief biographical sketch was drawn by an anonymous Royal Wootton Bassett artist in a coffee shop in the late 1990s and gifted to the poet.

The photograph preceding the 'Acknowledgements' section (page xix) is that of the terraced hills of Battir Village in Palestine. It is used with the courtesy of aicafe beit sahour – www.alternativenews.org

Introduction (page 1) – Vegetable Market in Nazareth, circa 1934-1937, Library of Congress (http://www.loc.gov/pictures/item/2007675860/)

The following sixteen illustrations are by the poet (title of the water colour followed by the title of its accompanying poem).

Acknowledgements

'Battir Village', Palestine, www.alternativenews.org

The poet is grateful to the following people and organisations for their help in locating sources and, where appropriate, for their permission to use resources where such permission is required:

Afridi, Sara of imeu.net

Staff of aicafe beit sahour (Alternative Information Centre).

Islam, Ramona L, Librarian, Harvard University Library, Harvard University, Cambridge, Massachusettes.

G., L. of the U.S. Copyright Office, Washington, DC.

Miller, Abigail, *The Tablet Magazine.*

S., W. S. of the U.S. Copyright Office, Washington DC.

Walsh, Dan, Curator of Palestine Poster Project Archives.

The poet is also grateful to many friends and colleagues, many of whom prefer to remain anonymous:

Eric Austen, Juman Karaman, Anna Killick and her Sixth Form Students, Lorna Low, Dave Martin, Dan Walsh and Susan Walpole.

As already stated, every possible effort has been made to acknowledge sources in the list of 'Illustrations' given above. If any reader notices any errors, omissions, potential copyright infringements or anything needing corrections, please contact the poet in order that the error may be amended immediately: fhm481812@aol.com

Introduction

'Vegetable Market in Nazareth', circa 1934-1937, Library of Congress,

http://www.loc.gov/pictures/item/2007675860/

Why do I write poetry? Why have I had the compulsion to

versify since my earliest childhood? What prompts these little

outpourings of words on a regular basis?

Our Palestinian history is as invisible as we have become.

Israel and its friends have created a new narrative which air brushes us out of the picture completely. Goebbels was right in asserting that "if you repeat a lie often enough, it becomes the truth". Israel had successfully established the idea of having a narrative. And it has become an absolute master at creating fictions that become, in time, permanent realities.

We Palestinians stand amazed when told that Palestine was "a land without a people for a people without a land" (Often cited by Zionist historians). Golda Meir, Prime Minister of Israel at the time, said, "There is no such a thing as a Palestinian people... It is not as if we came and threw them out and took their country. They didn't exist." (*The Sunday Times*, 15 June, 1969). This is an interesting statement from a woman who sent a postcard in 1930 to "Shoshana Golozinkit, Tel Aviv, Palestine!" (*The Jerusalem Post*, Saturday 8 March, 2014); that we are not there in the "myth that was Palestine" (Hunt, Dave, *Judgment Day, Islam, Israel and the Nations*, 2006).

These new truths are invariably supported by the notorious Israeli "facts on the ground" embellished by such claims as "incoming Jews making the desert bloom" and the indomitable "Zionists" successfully clearing "the Malaria infested swamps" ("It was only after the Zionists "made the desert bloom" that they [the Palestinians] became interested in taking it from us..." Levi Eshkol, Prime Minister of Israel, *Jerusalem Post*, February, 1969. "The country was mostly an empty desert, with only a few islands of Arab settlements; and Israel's cultivable land today was indeed redeemed from wilderness." Shimon Peres, President of Israel, *David's Sling: The Arming of Israel*, 1970. In April 2013 Peres also told Maariv: "I remember how it all began. The whole state of Israel is a millimetre of the whole Middle East. A statistical error, barren and disappointing land, swamps in the north, desert in the south, two lakes, one dead and overrated river. No natural resources apart from malaria. There was nothing here. And we now have the best agriculture in the world? This is a miracle: a land built by people.").

Palestinians stand wide eyed wondering how their very existence is shrouded in doubt despite us standing there in the flesh and blood.

I have often sat at lectures listening to history being re-written and, like some comic B movie about time travel, I and all my ancestors disappear or are transmogrified into so many other shapes: I have been urged to accept being a Jordanian, a Lebanese, a Syrian, an Arab, a Muslim from the Arabian Peninsula... anything but a Palestinian. I will ignore the utter insult of being urged to belong to countries that have maltreated my people, persecuted them and deprived them of any dignity beyond being indigent refugees in receipt of patronising sympathy. The 'free world' accepts these newly created narratives as if they were pure truths and lectures us Palestinians on restraint, on democracy, on compassion and on coexistence – in between supporting every engine of oppression against us under various names: guilt over the Holocaust, unquestioning Christian belief in *Old Testament* stories, greed, power, racism, colonial attitudes and many others. Meanwhile, we are either terrorists or, when peaceful,

4

unreasonable and possibly mad. I have found myself grateful to be called a little mad – a Palestinian who had lost his way… at least I was recognised as a Palestinian who must have existed somehow despite being told endlessly over the last sixty six years that my people and I never existed in these 'Malaria infested swamps'!

A few glaring examples would suffice. The prestigious British historian Sir Martin Gilbert tells us that in 1967 Israel kindly accepted to share its lands with Palestinians (Gilbert, *Israel: A History*, 2008, page xxi). This is a first time that I have seen invasion, occupation and repression described as a form of "sharing".

Christian Evangelists like Dave Hunt inform us that the Israelis kindly gave away Gaza "which historically belonged to her" and that the Arabs had attacked Israel in 1967 and that Israel was only defending itself against overwhelming odds (*thebereancall.org*, 'Israel and Prophetic Proof' Part II). He embellishes his sickening story by claiming to have been visiting Tyre in Lebanon at the time and telling us how he and his family begged the Lord for guidance...etc... Having been saved by the Lord as he escaped from Lebanon (a country not at all involved in the Six Day War) and having been delivered by the Lord into Syria (a country then at war with Israel), he then proceeds to defend every action by Israel despite the fact that "she" was at that time destroying three Arab armies, killing tens of thousands of Arabs and occupying more Palestinian lands as well as Egyptian and Syrian lands all of which, apart from Sinai, Israel still occupies ("The thesis that the danger of genocide was hanging over us in June 1967 and that Israel was fighting for its physical existence is only bluff, which was born and developed after the war." Israeli General Matityahu Peled, *Ha'aretz*, March 19, 1972). As in most of his so-called Christian articles, Hunt peppers his vapid argument with endless quotations from the Bible prophesying all kind of nonsense about Israel – as if a merciful and compassionate God would remotely support the dispossession, oppression and wholesale murder of a whole people for no reason other than His prima donnish jealousies and adolescent tantrums. Furthermore, Hunt fills his writings with offensive and virulent hatred of Islam.

Dershowitz is seriously quoted by Zionists and Christian Evangelists as a great scholar, even when his book *The Case for Israel* (2003) is as glaring a falsification of the world picture as that ridiculous work *The Protocols of the Elders of Zion* (almost certainly fabricated by the Russian secret police between 1897-1899 with a summary first published in 1903 – it was heavily used by White Russians later to discredit the Bolshevik Revolution which they attributed to the Jews – the similarities to today's Islamophobia are alarming). Such works would be funny if it were not for the fact that their pages are kept alive by the endless sufferings of the innocent at the hands of those who believe the virulent gibberish that they spout.

I remember asking a rather unsavoury near relation of mine why Hitler got away with his murderous thuggery when his sick political plans were there for all to see in his rambling and rather unreadable *Mein Kampf.* The man looked uncomfortable. His somewhat ill-educated and often secretly racist wife came to his rescue and explained: "But we did not know, dear, what was happening…". In my youthful zeal, I showed her copies of contemporary newspapers which I had collected as part of researching the Holocaust. I pointed to reports of particular events as they were happening: "Kristallnacht", the "Dachau" camp near supremely 'civilised' München (Munich) where Communists were sent during and after the "Night of the Long Knives", the Nuremberg speeches promulgating the detestable race laws… The husband, who had by then presumably gathered his overtly racist thoughts, stepped in to relieve his embarrassed wife by saying: "We laughed at Herr Hitler in those days. We made fun of his silly tooth brush moustache…". This is as feeble a response as another equally obnoxious relation of mine saying that Hitler "cured unemployment, made the trains run on time, kept streets safe for patriotic Germans…"

"What about the Jews? The Gypsies? The trade unionists?" asked I in my naïve youth. The relation concerned waved his hand dismissively just as Ben Gurion did when asked what was to be done with the Palestinians remaining behind Israeli lines (Yitzhak Rabin's *Memoires*, excluded when published but republished by the *New York Times* on 23 October 1979. Ben Gurion stated in a letter to his son dated 5 October 1937, "We must expel Arabs [Palestinians] and take their place"). The dismissive gesture was validated with the statement that "you don't build a great nation without spilling blood...". These people grow to believe their own lies in a way that brings George Orwell's *1984* world to life.

These lies are like theatre and, like all good theatre, they work superbly. Israel has even cleverly invented the wonderful tradition of new arrivals being urged to adopt new names rather like theatrical agents suggesting that actors with difficult names might wish to do, so that their potential fans could remember them better! These names give Israel's leaders historical credibility whilst accentuating their Jewish roots: David Gruen becomes David Ben Gurion, Golda Mabovitch becomes Golda Meir, Yitzhak Rubitzov becomes Yitzhak Rabin, Szymon Perski becomes Shimon Peres, Ariel Scheinermann becomes Ariel Sharon, Ehud Brog becomes Ehud Barak, Evet Lvovich Liberman becomes Avigdor Lieberman...etc... The notion is as bizarre as is the creation of a new State on the land of an already existing State by driving its people out, rewriting its history and creating new stories and facts on the ground to justify the original injustice. Changing East European and Russian names also both Judaises and homogenises Israel's new citizens and renascent Hebrew culture and language – probably Israel's most spectacular and, indeed, admirable success – in educational terms nothing short of a miracle.

I recently met an Evangelical Christian friend in a café. I asked her if she really believed the horrendous lies in the book that she was reading when I arrived (*From Time Immemorial* by Joan Peters – 1984). The book basically argues that Palestine was an empty land ready to welcome the Jews back to their homeland. My friend's eyes grew wide open as they always did whenever she spoke about her faith. She proceeded to give me a Messianic rant about *The Old Testament* 'Promise' and about the Jews returning home to an empty country. I sat there feeling a mounting sense of despair and a deep feeling of endless hurt when an alleged friend insensitively denies me my very existence because of her extreme religious views. I agreed with Ben Gurion when he said that he understood Palestinian anger because the God that promised him the Holy Land was not their God in the first place ("If I were an Arab leader, I would never sign an agreement with Israel. It is normal; we have taken their country. It is true God promised it to us, but how could that interest them? Our God is not theirs. There has been Anti-Semitism, the Nazis, Hitler, Auschwitz, but was that their fault? They see but one thing: we have come and we have stolen their country. Why should they accept that? They may perhaps forget in one or two generations' time, but for the moment there is no chance. So, it's simple: we have to stay strong and maintain a powerful army. Our whole policy is there. Otherwise the Arabs will wipe us out." Ben Gurion, 1956, Goldmann, Nahum, *The Jewish Pardox*, 1978, translated by Steve Cox). He (God) certainly was not mine to give my homeland away to European settlers. I asked my so-called friend to pinch me, to slap me, to punch me, to ship me off in cattle trains, to gas me... since I did not even exist as that being which I was born to be: a Palestinian. Not in her so-called Christian world – a world without an iota of Jesus Christ as I understand Him.

I suddenly realised the simple truth that all our evils come from within and that God was being used to justify any inhumanity that would strip us of our homeland for the convenience of others. I realised that we Palestinians had lost out to an evil but powerful hypocrisy, greed, acquisitive nationalism, evil beliefs linked to distorted faiths and an inhuman superiority of arms. We had lost to a people who themselves had been maltreated in a most pernicious and inhuman way – and who should know better than to exclude us Palestinians from their "never again" – a truly hard earned psychological makeup ("There is a huge gap between us and our enemies not just in ability but in morality, culture, sanctity of life, and conscience. They are our neighbours here, but it seems as if a distance of a few hundred meters away, there are people who do not belong to our continent, to our world, but actually belong to a different galaxy." Israeli President Moshe Katsav, *The Jerusalem Post*, May 10, 2001).

That tragic loss is why I write poetry: to make order out of chaos. To explain the inexplicable. To speak to my oppressors and to offer them the hand of peace and friendship. To give my Diaspora loneliness some meaning – some humanity – some compassion.

I can not and will not bear a gun.

I can not and will not hurt a fellow human being whatever s/he is or chooses to be or believe.

I deplore all violence and all acts of injustice.

So I draw out of its scabbard, not my sword, but my pen and I create little worlds of anger, hurt, upset, betrayal, love, friendship, peace and – most of all – forgiveness for pasts beyond our control any longer, and coexistence for futures in our hands if only we would.

Being a Palestinian is an existential impossibility...

We Palestinians have gone through so many changes over the last hundred years – and, indeed, before – that we no longer know who we are or what we are.

Those of us outside Palestine have been through various periods of disbelief at our dispossession. Disbelief soon made way to overwhelming amazement at a callous world that could not even see – let alone acknowledge – our refugee lives as a glaring injustice unparalleled in world history.

Our amazement was eventually displaced by a deep depression mired in hopeless despair. We stared about us questioning the obvious: "We suffer for reasons beyond our control. Why is the world so indifferent? What have we done to deserve this?" Most of us still suspect that this was precisely how Jews in Europe and Russia felt for decades before Israel was even thought of towards the end of the Nineteenth Century. Indeed, it is a callous modern irony that we Palestinians have paid a heavy price for European anti-Semitism at the hands of its very victims. We have become the new Jews – with the world's eyes firmly averted away from our dolorous existence – and, to many, non-existence (The Palestinians are "beasts walking on two legs... Our race is the Master Race. We are divine gods on this planet. We are as different from inferior races as they are from insects. In fact, compared to our race, other races are beasts and animals, cattle at best. Other races are considered as human excrement. Our destiny is to rule over the inferior races. Our earthly kingdom will be ruled by our leader with a rod of iron. The masses will lick our feet and serve us as our slaves." Menachem Begin, Israeli Prime Minister, speech to the Knesset, *New Statesman*, June 25, 1982). Such nasty sentiments are reiterated by extreme Rabbis such as Rabbi Ovadia Yosef.

When no answer to our desperate questions came, our depression predictably became anger, rage and then defiance. This last was effectively our undoing. It was an adolescent defiance that caused us to resist occupation and oppression by fighting endless proxy wars everywhere other than in Palestine itself. We, since 1917, collected endless unworthy friends who constantly betrayed us and turned their fury against us whilst we cheerfully supported endless immoral losers such as Hitler, Saddam Hussein, Iranian Revolutionaries hell bent on self destruction, Syrian dictators who starved us, Egyptian recidivists whose promises turned to murderous persecution in Gaza... The list is endless. Amidst this apocalyptic defiance we had no leaders worthy of the name, no visionaries, no Nelson Mandela figures whose foresight and compassion could help us negotiate with the only conceivable partner available to us: the Israelis.

And defiance took many forms: ranting, raving, lashing out at anyone, fighting each other, making alliances with extremists, seeking a strategy for self-preservation, seeking power wherever it may be available, becoming obsessive about education as the only way out of our misery, finding solutions in the most inappropriate places including religion, embracing obscurantism, nepotism and any consoling -ism floating by...

Those of our Palestinian compatriots who lived on in the Occupied Territories went through similar experiences and sensations with a few additions because of their particular circumstances. Along with disbelief, amazement, depression, despair, anger, rage, defiance in all their forms, they also faced authoritarian Jordanian rule, oppressive Israeli occupation, daily humiliations, crushing military rule, imprisonment, judicial killings, bombings, regular arrests and detention, imposed poverty... (Israeli Prime Minister, Yitzhak Shamir, issued a stark warning to Palestinians waging the Intifada: "...rioters would be crushed "like grasshoppers"... We say to them from the heights of this mountain and from the perspective of thousands of years of history that they are like grasshoppers to us... [They] will have [his] head smashed against boulders and walls." *New York Times*, April 1, 1988.)

Eventually, these Palestinian populations were divided into ones living in two huge open air prisons called the 'West Bank' and 'Gaza' both ruled by unconscionable and inefficient Palestinian administrations. In Gaza, in Southern Palestine, Palestinians continue to suffer a crippling siege that deprives them of the very basic amenities of their daily necessities. Israel is helped by the Egyptian military which had ousted the first democratically elected President in its history. The

Egyptians appear determined to starve Gaza's Palestinians into cowering submission. They have blocked crossings, designated Hamas a "terrorist organisation" and have stepped up their customary persecution of Palestinian refugees unfortunate enough to be living in Egypt. It is not clear why Gaza's Palestinians apparently need to be crushed so abominably by their two inimical neighbours – Israel and Egypt. In Eastern Palestine (variously known as the 'West Bank' or the 'Occupied Territories' in yet another attempt to excise the very name Palestine out of human history), the Palestinians there have, to a point, given in to the occupation by Israel. After almost forty seven years, Israel's grip on Eastern Palestine is stronger than ever with over half a million illegally settled Jews living on stolen prime land and thus becoming Israel's new "facts on the ground" to create another huge demographic change ("When we have settled the land, all the Arabs will be able to do about it will be to scurry around like drugged cockroaches in a bottle." Raphael Eitan, Chief of Staff of the IDF, *New York Times*, April, 14, 1983. "Everybody has to move, run and grab as many hilltops as they can to enlarge the settlements because everything we take now will stay ours. Everything we don't grab will go to them." Ariel Sharon, Israeli Defence Minister, Foreign Minister, Prime Minister, Agence France Presse, November, 15, 1998).

Given the other "fact on the ground" of the inconvenience of a Palestinian population living there since time immemorial, it does not take a genius of history to see what is inevitably coming. At best, these Palestinians will join the one and a half million "Arabushim" living as second class citizens inside pre-1967 Israel which is itself a land mass which includes some 30% of historical Palestine forcibly occupied after the Palestinians and their so-called Arab allies rejected the impractical United Nations division of 1947 – a division that had a Palestine and an Israel criss crossing each other at various points in a ridiculous arrangement of three sections each that could not possibly be remotely functional as two states with non-contiguous lands. Just below the best scenario would be a minute canton of unconnected Palestinian Bantustans under Israeli control for decades and generations to come – a peace deal which would clearly favour Israel and which, as ever, the United States is complicit in orchestrating with staggering bare-faced and mind boggling hypocrisy ("Every time we do something you tell me America will do this and will do that. I want to tell you something very clear: Don't worry about American pressure on Israel. We, the Jewish people, control America, and the Americans know it." Ariel Sharon, Israeli Prime Minister, speaking to Shimon Peres, October 5, 2001, *Kol Yisrael Radio*).

Israeli Prime Minister Netanyahu, "apparently not knowing that his words were being recorded" (*The Washington Post*, reporter Glenn Kessler, July 16, 2010), also said "I know what America is. America is a thing you can move very easily, move it in the right direction. They won't get in the way." (*The Washington Post*, reporter Glenn Kessler, July 16, 2010). *The Washington Post* further reports that "Netanyahu also bragged how he undercut the peace process when he was prime minister during the Clinton administration. 'They asked me before the election if I'd honor [the Oslo Accords],' he said. 'I said I would, but... I'm going to interpret the accords in such a way that would allow me to put an end to this galloping forward to the '67 borders. How do we do it? Nobody said what defined military zones were. Defined military zones are security zones; as far as I'm concerned, the entire Jordan Valley is a defined military zone. Go argue.'" (*The Washington Post*, reporter Glenn Kessler, July 16, 2010). The recording concerned led the Israeli journalist Gideon Levy to remark, "This video should have been banned for broadcast to minors. This video should have been shown in every home in Israel, then sent to Washington and Ramallah. Banned for viewing by children so as not to corrupt them, and distributed around the country and the world so that everyone will know who leads the government of Israel". (*Haaretz*, July 15, 2010). The 2001 recording shows a relaxed Netanyahu speaking to illegal Jewish Settlers in Palestine and assuring them that the Palestinians will be dealt with, "The main thing, first of all, is to hit them. Not just one blow, but blows that are so painful that the price will be too heavy to be borne." (youtube.com – 'America Is Easy to Push Around'. Search under 'DN! Netanyahu in 2001, US Won't Get in the Way of Israeli Expansionism').

The worst scenario, which is the probable one as is evidenced by current global politics, religious extremism, Western double standards and other recent developments, will be a repeat of the ethnic cleansing of Palestine in 1947 and 1948 through intimidation, murder and wholesale expulsions ("How can we return the occupied territories? There is nobody to return them to." Golda Meir, March 8, 1969, Lilienthal, Alfred, *The Zionist Connection II: What Price Peace*, 1978. "We must do everything to insure they never do return. The old will die and the young will forget." David Ben-Gurion's Diary, 18 July, 1948, Michael Bar Zohar, *Ben-Gurion: The Armed Prophet*, 1967).

Indeed, Israel had always claimed that there is already a Palestine called Jordan. In other words, the Jordanian people are being told to hand over their territory to newly arrived Palestinians so that they can then live in peace under an illiberal, autocratic and unelected government. This ethnic cleansing is already happening through the creation of 'Jews only' areas in many parts of the occupied 'West Bank' and through the 'Judaisation' of Jerusalem and other areas.

Palestinians living in these occupied areas (designated "territories" in order to avoid any association with nationhood, i.e. Palestine), have become so accustomed to being occupied that they adopt an utterly fatalistic approach as shown by a great deal that they say and do ("We have to kill all the Palestinians unless they are resigned to live here as slaves." Chairman Heilburn of the Committee for the Re-election of General Shlomo Lahat, The Mayor of Tel Aviv, October 1983).

A Palestinian student living under Israeli occupation speaks for many when he says:

> I know you would have expected us as Palestinians to tell you about our lives, and how Israel has ruined everything for us, and killed our friends and families. But that's not the case. Yes when we hear and see our beloved Palestinians die, we feel or I feel like somebody just ripped my heart out of my chest (and I'm not exaggerating about how I feel), but that does not stop us from moving on. Instead it motivates us even more to continue our education in order to help Palestine to become once and for all FREE! Yes it hurts me so much to see settlements from my window, or to be specific, from my school ground, it is like so clear from our school. And yes it hurts me even more that I have to get an approval or permission from

Israeli people in order to get into Jerusalem, Akka, **** (which is where I'm originally from, but NEVER been there). It does hurt, words can't even describe how I feel, but we don't live on remembering the past, or wishing things were different. Our role in this world is to live a life of love and happiness, because no power in this world will take that from us. If it had to come down to one thing that the Israeli people taught us, it will surely be LOVE. I actually have a lot to share…

Such sentiments from the new generation of Palestinians give me hope…

Aspirations for freedom aside, life continues as normal in occupied Palestine partly because it has to and partly because Israel has created the reality that makes it so despite the repressive occupation. Another Palestinian living in Ramallah shows how, despite being occupied, her life is relatively normal:

…the conflict does not make my life very different from anyone anywhere else in the world, but it does often create huge obstacles for things like transportation and the freedom of expression. This is probably because I live in Ramallah which is not very involved in the direct confrontations between the two sides;

however, many Palestinians do have to go through horrible experiences just to get through an ordinary day.

In other words, the economy is relatively buoyant in Ramallah and so, by the grace of the occupier, Palestinians can live in relative comfort as long as "they behave themselves" as a moderate Israeli so eloquently put it. Indeed, these Palestinians do "behave themselves" by facilitating the occupation as witnessed by a Diaspora Palestinian visiting Nablus:

One new development I have found in this visit is the very general loss of interest to indulge in any discussion of any political, military, or occupational matters of the region, or even of the local community with municipalities of Palestinian towns elected less than a year ago... Rather, people in general were more focused on their individual and at the same time, controversial concerns on issues related to economy: their own family's financial situation, how to make more money, and entertainment. This self-centred attitude, and shift from interest in national matters to the family microcosm only, was never the norm in the West Bank society that I am familiar with. I also find it difficult to explain because these new areas of interest are directly impacted by the wider circle of factors related to the occupation, yet one

> commonly senses something of a denial to
> make this link, and a preference to busy
> themselves with whims of which new
> restaurant to try/ car to buy/ shopping to do
> inside Palestine of 1948!

Another Palestinian wrote to me responding to an article that I had written on the role of integrated education in creating peace between Israelis and Palestinians. She agreed with my sentiments but warned of her deep feeling of pessimism after having just visited the West Bank. She felt that this deniability of occupation was coupled with economic needs as well as economic greed amongst the occupied Palestinians. She described what she had witnessed during her visit. The following is a faithful summary of what she wrote.

During the Ramadan Eid in 2013, Israel made over 100 million Israeli Sheqels (29,000,000.00 US Dollars – 17,000,000.00 British Pounds) from Palestinians travelling into Israel proper after obtaining special permits over three days that allowed them to cross the Green Line and shop interminably. Special buses were laid on to transport them across the Green Line to spend money that most did not even have since the main payment methods were credit cards – clear hostage to fortune in an ailing Palestinian economy.

A young Palestinian writes of his deep sadness as he surveys "dazzling and wide fields" destroyed by "settlements, checkpoints, and barriers that prevent me from reaching" the fields so sought after. He describes his life in a Palestinian town as being "normal" but regrets his inability to visit "occupied cities" in Israel because he does not have the necessary permit. He speaks eloquently about his sadness at not being able to visit his family home because it is now lived in by "Jews" and Palestinians are actively excluded from the area. Another young Palestinian speaks quite fatalistically about her inability to visit anywhere in "Areas B or C" without an Israeli permit which she claims is rarely granted and which, when granted, takes an inordinately long time.

Another Palestinian student says that life under occupation is "so boring because there's nothing to do other than going to coffee shops and restaurants and of course we can't visit places other than the West Bank like Jaffa or Haifa where there are lots of parks, shopping centres and of course a lot of beaches because the Israelis forbid it and have endless checkpoints to discourage any travel…"

These are only a small sample of Palestinian youngsters living under occupation in precisely the way that any young person lives anywhere in the world – except for the amazing fatalism that makes them accept their lot as inevitable. Although peace loving and self-sufficient by necessity, theirs is a tragic existence since there is apparently little light at the end of the tunnel and a peaceful co-existence with Israel is currently not even on their horizon. They are making the best of a bad job. Not much has changed since 1983 when Rafael Eitan, Chief of Staff of the IDF said: "We declare openly that the Arabs have no right to settle on even one centimetre of Eretz Israel… We shall use the ultimate force until the Palestinians come crawling to us on all fours." (*New York Times*, April 14, 1983).

Another group of Palestinians is made of some one and a half million Palestinians living in pre-1967 Israel. They are the "Arabushim" so marginalised by Israel despite being its alleged 'citizens'. They suffer all the indignities heaped on second class citizens anywhere in the world. Their schools are underfunded. Their areas are indifferently served by their local municipalities. In many areas, the contrast between the first world living luxury of European, Arab and other Jews in Israel is starkly contrasted with the relative poverty and squalor of third world living by Palestinian Israelis. They also suffer the most terrifying race laws since Hitler's Nuremberg laws. Indeed, the experience of Palestinians within Israel goes counter to every pretence that Israeli society wishes the world to see of its civilised Jewish norms. (Indeed, Ariel Sharon expressed great impatience with Israel's 'pure' image because he felt tired of being accused of waging "a dirty war": "We'll hear no more of that nonsense about the unique Jewish morality. No more talk about a unique people being a light upon the nations. No more uniqueness and no more sweetness and light. Good riddance." *Davar*, December 17, 1982). These civilised norms do exist, but only for Jews. Recently, the Knesset has promulgated a law that allows the same rights to Israeli Palestinian Christians (who, according to Israel, are not really Arabs anyhow – since Arabs are Muslims who are professed enemies of Israel). Many Israeli friends and colleagues write movingly of the isolation of Israeli Palestinians professing a Muslim faith. Almost everyone who is of Palestinian origin always specifically requests that they are not to be quoted in any of my writings for fear of repercussions. This is the new anti-Semitism. Palestinians are also descendants of Abraham and his Bondswoman Hagar to whose son Ishmael God promised greatness and glory. If the current Arab situation on the ground is a result of this so-called Promise, then God must have a spectacularly quirky sense of humour!

A good Israeli friend has suggested that Arabs in general and Palestinians in particular were not the descendants of Abraham. They were purely the descendants of an invading Islamic horde that streamed northwards from the Arabian Peninsula and stole the land, lived there until the land was liberated by Israel.

A Christian friend cheerfully agreed with this analysis and added that what befell the Palestinians may have been sad but that it was inevitable as a result of the sins of their fathers who occupied the land in the first place. When I suggested that what happened to us Palestinians does take the concept of "the sins of the fathers" a little far, she insisted that this was the case and that it was purely God's will which we Palestinians were now called upon to accept as part of "coming to the Lord". I tried to paint a picture of Palestinian suffering and dared compare it to what happened to Jews in Europe. Another Israeli friend objected to this comparison saying that there was no equivalence whatever. I desperately wanted to know what one would say to a Palestinian mother who had lost her child, to a Palestinian family watching their house being demolished to make way for 'Jews only' areas, to a Gazan living in squalor as if s/he were living in medieval times, to the tens of thousands of Palestinians who have died since 1948 and to the millions living in abject poverty in camps around the Arab world and inside the Occupied Territories... My Israeli friend wanted me to accept that their suffering was less than that of the Jews – apartheid lives even beyond the grave.

"O reason not the need! Our basest beggars
Are in the poorest things superfluous.
Allow not nature more than nature needs,
Man's life is as cheap as beast's."

We Palestinians are as King Lear – and Bedlam is our lot in this world of indifference, cruelty, force and double standards.

These rules only apply to us and no one else.

Of course, there is yet another cohort of Palestinians who have now been naturalised American, British, French, German and many other nationalities. I have always found my "Naturalisation" papers delightfully amusing given Shakespeare's use of the term 'natural' as being "a fool" or "a simpleton". On balance these days, I would rather be a British "fool" than an Arab one despite being severely reprimanded for saying this by many Arab family and friends. But then my observations of the vast hypocrisy that both Arabs and the Western world evince in their dealings with Palestinians, the truth is that I have reached a stage where I couldn't care less what any of such two faced alleged persons of faith think about me or my country.

As a Palestinian, my biggest difficulty has always been the staggering hypocrisy of the Western world when it comes to Palestine. I have become almost neurotic about what I hear – or, more often, about what I do not hear – from the leaders of the so-called "free world". I often wonder if I am the only person who cringes with sheer disgust when I hear Cameron, Hague, Obama, Kerry, Merkel and so many others talk about justice, decency, democracy, humanity and all things so precious to our freedoms. Precious and necessary – except, of course, when it comes to us Palestinians.

I shudder to hear Kerry pontificating about the right of people for self determination and peaceful existence (except, presumably, for Palestinians under occupation). I cringe to hear Hague lecturing the Russians about the rights of their neighbours to their territorial integrity and national sovereignty (except, as it were, for the Palestinians who should be pleased to be under Israeli occupation). I feel positively sick hearing Bush Senior lecturing that abominable man Saddam Hussein about the immorality of occupying Kuwait (but not a whisper to

Israel about the immorality of occupying Palestinian lands). My stomach turns when I hear Obama lecture Egyptians on the need for restraint and on democratic values (not a hint of any such restraint when it comes to Israelis maltreating oppressed Palestinians). Cameron's hypocrisy is dizzying when he prefaces his condemnation of Israel for abusing British passports used by those Israeli agents involved in murdering a Palestinian in Dubai by saying that he had always been a "friend of Israel" and always would be. The examples of such double standards are so many that alone they would fill several volumes just to list. Perhaps the most spectacular is the pretence of the Israeli Army's "purity of arms" – tell that to Palestinians in Sabra and Shatila, in Gaza, in Jenin, in Deir Yassin, in Jordan, in the West Bank…etc…

Obama can not bring himself to lead by telling Israel to "pack it in". Enough is enough. He feels that he has to mollify the Israelis by appealing to their better self. Making a speech in occupied Jerusalem which is not recognised by any country in the world as the "capital of Israel", he pleads with them:

> Put yourself in their shoes – look at the world
> through their eyes. It is not fair that a
> Palestinian child cannot grow up in a state of
> her own, and lives with the presence of a
> foreign army that controls the movements of
> her parents, every single day…

Acknowledging that Israel's is "a foreign army" occupying

Palestine, all he can do is try to make the occupier see sense.

He can not get himself to have the moral courage to say, "Get

out and get out now or else!" For a world leader of, allegedly,

the most powerful nation on earth, he always appears to

implore Israel in a staggeringly ignominious manner whilst

presidentially directing and ordering everyone else including

countries significantly more powerful than little Israel – e.g.

Russia, China, India and other emerging powers. Some

Palestinians are not surprised by this state of affairs, since, as

Ariel Sharon asserted, "We, the Jewish people, control

America". It may be that AIPAC is politically very influential in

Washington. It may even be that Jewish voters make or break

a President. The real reason is more likely to be that President

Obama is displaying amazing moral cowardice with no

substantial legacy to be left behind after he departs his weak

and ineffective Presidency.

Indeed, as I write this piece, my heart goes out to the Ukrainian people suffering under their giant bully of a neighbour. I agree with NATO that Russia's behaviour violates every principle of the United Nations. I agree with the British Government and the US President in condemning Russia.

What sickens me to the point of despair is the fact that Israel had done the same and infinitely worse to Palestinians without a murmur from those very same representatives of freedom, democracy, decency, compassion, Christianity... This conspiracy of silence is absolutely terrifying to us Palestinians. What have we done to deserve this?

It is ironic that the only people who remotely understand and acknowledge the injustice done to Palestinians are Israelis who, as Jews, know about suffering yet, ironically, choose to impose it on another people in the name of their own redemption.

The Holocaust was an indescribable crime. It happened partly because the rest of the world looked the other way. Neither I nor my ancestors were responsible for it. The Europeans perpetrated it and we Palestinians are paying for it. That is patently wrong and unjust.

Many Israelis recognise this but their voices are drowned by extremists and by an indifferent and hypocritical Western World.

An American Jew, Michelle Cohen Corasanti, author of *The Almond Tree*, wrote a response to President Obama's patronising and rather sickening Jerusalem speech. She started off by telling Obama that many Jews had forgotten their history. They had forgotten that the Nazis had told them evil was in their blood before they proceeded to steal their property, arrest them, ghettoise and kill them. She suggested that in order to do what Obama wanted and put herself in Palestinian shoes, all that had to happen was to remember recent Jewish past:

These are the lessons the Holocaust taught me: We must never be bystanders to human suffering. "Never again" means never again for any people ever again. When the horrors of the Holocaust were uncovered, there was a need to find a place for the survivors to go. The west , didn't want us so they were happy to give us Palestine. And they were happy the buy the fallacy that Palestine was "a land without a people for a people without a land", and that we made the desert bloom. Let's be honest, Palestine already had people, the Palestinians, and the vast majority of whom were not Jewish. Jerusalem, Bethlehem, Acre, Haifa, Nazareth, Jaffa and many more cities were already well-developed. These cities were made of stone and contained universities, hospitals, schools, tea houses and hotels. There were trains, sea ports and international trade and travel. The desert we brought to bloom was the land on which we built Tel Aviv in 1909, and that's it.

She goes on to ask Obama to be honest and see the truth for what it is, "The Palestinians have paid the price for the Holocaust".

The main Jewish tenet is one of not doing to others that which is hateful to a Jew. Michelle Cohen Corasanti quotes Rabbi Hillel as asserting this overriding moral principle at the heart of Judaism. It is also at the heart of Christianity – although listening to those Christians who support Israel would lead one to believe that Christ never made *The Sermon on Mount* since what has happened to the Palestinians would make Him weep. But then, those Christians have abused the message of both *Old* and *New* *Testaments* deplorably to justify every evil committed in the name of the faith that they pretend to have.

Michelle Cohen Corasanti went further and put herself in the shoes of a Palestinian in writing *The Almond Tree* using a Palestinian voice. 'The Almond Tree' became a powerful project for peace which had wide repercussions and involved many prominent Americans, Israelis and Palestinians.

Even warlike Israelis who caused us Palestinians a great deal of suffering accept that we were dispossessed:

> "Jewish villages were built in the place of Arab villages. You do not even know the names of these Arab villages, and I do not blame you because geography books no longer exist. Not only do the books not exist, the Arab villages are not there either. Nahlal arose in the place of Mahlul; Kibbutz Gvat in the place of Jibta; Kibbutz Sarid in the place of Huneifis; and Kefar Yehushua in the place of Tal al-Shuman. There is not a single place built in this country that did not have a former

Arab population." Moshe Dayan, *Haaretz*, 4
April 1969.

There are many other Jews who speak in a similarly brave manner from Miko Peled to Illan Pappe to Noam Chomsky to Noam Chayut (*The Girl Who Stole My Holocaust*) and many others.

These are the courageous people who give me some hope despite my deeply rooted sense of despair and outrage. Their voices may be largely drowned by the roar of warmongers, expansionists and rejectionists in both Israel and Palestine. But their message is uncompromising. What happened to us Palestinians was an injustice that should be rectified forthwith.

I have written extensively on the potential for peace between us Palestinians and Israelis. This has subjected me to the most pernicious responses from both Israelis and Palestinians. To the Palestinians I am, at best, naïve, and, at worst, a traitor willing to sleep with the enemy. To the Israelis, I am, at best, a genuine chap who really does want peace, to, at worst, a manipulator trying to undermine Israel by clever means –

"playing us at our game" as one Israeli commentator wrote:

> You forget that we are masters at this game
> of obfuscating, cover ups, hand wringing and
> other such superb ploys that the West so
> readily believes partly because they are
> stupid and partly because they love Israel
> because it has helped them get rid of the
> hated Jews. (Letter to the poet)

There is a great deal of truth in this last statement. Winston

Churchill considered himself a Zionist without specifically

being able to pinpoint where such a development came from:

"I am a Zionist, let me make that clear. I was one of the

original ones after *The Balfour Declaration* and I have worked

faithfully for it" (Churchill speaking at the Washington Press

Club, 1954).

He also said, rather significantly in defence of Jewish right to

settle in Palestine:

> I do not admit that the dog in the manger has
> the final right to the manger, even though he
> may have lain there for a very long time. I do
> not admit, for instance, that a great wrong

has been done to the Red Indians of America, or the black people of Australia. I do not think the Red Indians had any right to say, 'The American Continent belongs to us and we are not going to have any of these European settlers coming in here'. They had not the right, nor had they the power. (Churchill giving evidence before the *Palestine Royal Commission* known as *The Peel Commission*, 1937).

Churchill put such a rationale within an argument of the supremacy of the white races over the indigenous ones:

I do not admit that a wrong has been done to these people by the fact that a stronger race, a higher-grade race, a more worldly wise race to put it that way, has come in and taken their place" (Ibid).

Yet Churchill did go on to warn that the creation of Israel would lead to decades of confrontation in the Middle East – clearly accepting that an injustice had been done to the Palestinians:

The position of the hundreds of thousands of Arabs [Palestinians] driven from their homes and existing precariously in the no-man's-land created round Israel's frontiers is cruel and dangerous (Churchill, Winston, *The Second World War*, Epilogue, 1957).

Of course, such contradictory utterances by Churchill must be put side by side with his bizarre reasoning for supporting the creation of the State of Israel. In his article in *The Illustrated Sunday Herald*, February 8, 1920 'Zionism versus Bolshevism: A Struggle for the Soul of the Jewish People', Churchill places the responsibility for Bolshevism on the shoulders of Russian Jews:

> Some people like Jews and some do not; but no thoughtful man can doubt the fact that they are beyond all question the most formidable and the most remarkable race which has ever appeared in the world. And it may well be that this same astounding race may at the present time be in the actual process of producing another system of morals and philosophy, as malevolent as Christianity was benevolent, which, if not arrested would shatter irretrievably all that Christianity has rendered possible. It would almost seem as if the gospel of Christ and the gospel of Antichrist were destined to originate among the same people; and that this mystic and mysterious race had been chosen for the supreme manifestations, both of the divine and the diabolical.

In order to resolve what Churchill perceived as the destabilising influence of the Jews, he ends his outrageously anti-Semitic article by suggesting that a Jewish State would resolve this difficult conundrum of a great people causing such

damage in Russia – giving credence to the argument that

Western support for Israel emanated more from wishing to be

rid of their Jewish communities than it did from any sense of

decency, humanity or empathy for a long suffering people:

> Zionism offers the third sphere to the political
> conceptions of the Jewish race. In violent
> contrast to international communism, Zionism
> has already become a factor in the political
> convulsions of Russia, as a powerful
> competing influence in Bolshevik circles with
> the international communistic system.
> Nothing could be more significant than the
> fury with which Trotsky has attacked the
> Zionists generally, and Dr. Weissmann in
> particular. The cruel penetration of his mind
> leaves him in no doubt that his schemes of a
> world-wide communistic State under Jewish
> domination are directly thwarted and
> hindered by this new ideal, which directs the
> energies and the hopes of Jews in every land
> towards a simpler, a truer, and a far more
> attainable goal. The struggle which is now
> beginning between the Zionist and Bolshevik
> Jews is little less than a struggle for the soul
> of the Jewish people.

I, as a Palestinian, have long ago come to conclusion that we

had no allies, no friends and no sympathisers. We are invisible

to the majority of the world. The Arab world has abandoned us utterly as it continues full time in that which it is best at: Inept governance, oppression, suppression of personal freedoms, self-destruction and obscurantism tinged with greed and the unthinking aping of everything that the West does regardless of its merits or otherwise. Israel sees us as irrelevant – at best a nuisance to its grand plan ("One million Arabs are not worth a Jewish fingernail." Rabbi Yaacov Perrin, *New York Times*, February 28, 1994). The West prefers not to discuss our predicament – it salves its conscience by creating United Nations organisations that feed and clothe Palestinian refugees all over the Arab world. The United Nations throws out endless Resolutions in our favour (including the Right of Return to Palestine and condemnation of Israel's occupation) ("If the General Assembly were to vote by 121 votes to 1 in favour of "Israel" returning to the armistice line [pre-June 1967] "Israel" would refuse to comply with the decision." Abba Eban, Israeli diplomat, Minister of Foreign Affairs, Deputy Prime Minister, *New York Times*, June, 19, 1967). These Resolutions have all been utterly ignored by the Israel (with blind American support in every single case). We as a people are fragmented, divided and suspicious of each other. We are easily manipulated by host countries or by allegedly humane donors. We lack democratic institutions and have made an absolute art of missing opportunities. We lack any worthwhile leadership. Sadly, the list of negative qualities associated with our recent history is so very long.

What we do have and always have had are two qualities: A strong abiding love of Palestine which, after sixty seven years of oppression, dispossession and persecution we have not given up on. We are deeply rooted in the Palestinian landscape and always will be whatever horrors are imposed on us and perpetrated by Israel as it "modernises" our backward existence and distorts our environment into its current ugly state and whatever may be the shortcomings that we display in our own daily national life. Secondly, we are lovers of the word, hence our love of books, of education, of reading and of writing. We are not fighters. We are not cynics. We are not planners. We are not civilised or even pretend to be or even wish to be if the West is an example of civilisation. We are story tellers, artists and poets. We have a lust for life. We wish to live in peace on our lands as we have done for hundreds of years. We, the gullible and simple 'savages' so abused by the Arabs, the Ottomans, the British, the Israelis, wish to return to our homes and to be left alone...

Our only weapon is the pen – now the keyboard as we become more and more ICT literate.

And being almost naturally literate in more than one way, we can write.

As I said at the beginning of this essay:

> I can not and will not bear a gun.
>
> I can not and will not hurt a fellow human being whatever s/he is or chooses to believe.
>
> I deplore all violence and all acts of injustice.
>
> So I draw out of its scabbard, not my sword, but my pen and I create little worlds of anger, hurt, upset, betrayal, love, friendship, peace and – most of all – forgiveness for pasts beyond our control any longer and coexistence for futures in our hands if only we would.

These are such poems. They help me cope with my tragic personal Diaspora in a cruel and indifferent world. Their kaleidoscopic words are my very Palestinian days connected each to each with abiding hope.

Painting, 'Alone', by the poet.

Credo

"Io credo in Dio,

Padre Omnipotente,

Creatore del cielo e della terra.

E in Gesù Cristo, suo unico Figlio, nostre Signore"…

There are mornings when even God is not sufficient solace.

"Be angry but do not blaspheme…"

Tortuous words that take us here and there, tear us apart and leave us

in a heap

Unthinking, unable to see for the endless threads that connect us each

to each

Blinding our morns with darkness and blighting our joys.

And this was such a morning for reasons beyond repair.

I sat staring into space wondering which corner was the wrong one.

And if I had taken that other corner, where would I be now?

And if God knew where, then why did He not put a simple signpost up?

'Cause He couldn't be fucking arsed to have any analytical response

get in the way

Of His little scheme "*moving in mysterious ways His wonders to*

perform".

I looked at my desk and there stood Dickens, De Kock and their

friends,

Beside them stood all my plans started almost forty years ago.

A lifetime of waste and inaction searching for the invisible

And striving for the unattainable – thus to this juncture;

After missing many crossroads and turning many corners.

"*So, what next?*" asked my inner voice without reprehension.

"*Where to? Which corner now?*"

And, as when a little child, before becoming a little man, I stepped out into the garden,

In search of solace to lighten my heart and mend my fractured soul.

I searched methodically with my outward eye and fed its inward tearful brother

For later reflection before deciding on how to smile.

There were pretty flowers, green green grass, luscious trees,

Some pretty wild growths swaying in the wind

And, of course, my favourite friends, the tree branches;

Their arms outstretched in supplication to the Heavens above,

Like my heart, hoping for some unattainable joy.

And there, before my eyes swayed a little – so little – tree.

It sprang from nowhere, it would seem, and stood by its parent.

I tried to name it but could not for I hate naming as it takes the joy away.

The baby tree swayed gently to and fro near my right foot

And I wondered what miracle would soon make it stand towering over me.

But in my inner eye, it will always be that little babe

Swaying childishly, without fear, little knowing its crossroads are full of woes

Just like mine had been and then I realised – as I always do when I stand in my garden.

"*Io credo in Dio,*

Padre Omnipotente,

Creatore del cielo e della terra.

E in Gesù Cristo, suo unico Figlio, nostre Signore"…

For what else is there to link my days each to each

So that they have meaning, fullness and all that

Makes life worthwhile – mend my soul,

Salve my heart and calm my mind;

With endless joys of natural beauty that tells me;

"*Whatever crossroad you took – it all led to this.*

And this, and only this, is all that matters in life and death.

Beauty beyond end and a loving heart without fear.

You have done no wrong and no wrong was done you."

And the baby tree was called - Palestine;

Where I no longer am

For the crosswords are heavily mined,

And no turning could there be.

Painting, 'Apartheid', by the poet.

Cycle

Well that was the way that was.

One thousand and seven hundred and quelque

A woman gave birth à la caesarean.

The cutting motion became her son's name.

The Miqdad. He who was "*untimely ripped*" and all that

Soon to be stolen by William and his Hathaway

To whom he bequeathed his bed

Which was used once with lovelessness instead.

So that one thousand and seven hundred and quelque

His chattel and other become the belongings to him

To wit El Miqdadi.

Which by and by a revolutionary in a British jail in the land in between

the two rivers

Mesopotamia

Iraq to you and I

Declared

"Let there be El Miqdadi henceforth".

And the middle class arse changed the 'q' to 'k'

Because it would be easier

So Mikdadi.

What a boring story.

Like Palestine's history.

God damn this world for boring us so

And making its game the boredom of the very game.

God damn this world for taking away all our aim

And calling it mercy by any other name.

It was.

It was, that is, until in Gosport town

Another revolutionary

Settled down and fell in love

With a Walpole

Of the north folk.

And all history became one

Indivisible

Inalienable

And eternal

Bright futures brighter pasts do make

You have used it before you damn fake

But it's true

Believe me my little - - -

Brighter futures brighter pasts do make.

Painting, 'Beach Walk', by the poet.

$E=MC^2$

I have always found it almost impossible to understand Einstein's

meaning of Relativity.

Still keenly interested I bought and read both volumes in 1980.

I well remember that day

For then I became the genius that I am not

And went home to sit in the garden and read

The secrets of the universe

Had a barbecue and played with two podgy infants

Blowing huge bubbles with Auntie Jessie

Whose Irishness made my very words melt into Joycean chamber

music

Which actually was about someone pissing into a pot.

But I digress.

This happens when you are a genius.

A diarrhoea of words.

So, *"the only justification for our concepts and system of concepts is*

that they serve to represent the complex of our experience; beyond

this they have no legitimacy".

I agree. I have often said that before. Many times.

And made it sound so fine

In Irish in our own land of Palestine.

Ergo, easy peasy: a physics theory is basically the construction of a

theoretical model of the world of physics and that model then embodies a system of concepts so that it serves to represent *"the complex of our experiences"*.

Reader, are you still with me or has your brain benumbed itself into blissful slumber?

"The complex of our experiences!"
Do you understand? Do you see? Do you not feel?

So we have congruence, constancy, bodies of reference, space of reference, time;
An 'x' here and an 'x' there followed by space belonging to body A
Moving towards body B.

There, it really is that easy.

But then, there is the difficulty, we produce a finite but unbounded universe.
We produce a series of wonderful contradictions
That then make flat beings with flat implements.

Cogito ergo sum – or is it?

I read and re-read Einstein.

I decorated my stairs with his books.

I must be the only English literature doctor who loves physics

And understands neither it nor English literature.

I even went to Bern and rode on the tram looking for tall creatures and

bent buildings

And pretended that I loved a member of the royal household

Whom I impregnated with a schizophrenic mathematical genius

And left to live with my slippers in Massachusetts.

Then, epiphany of epiphanies (aye, me is spiritual too)

I understood it all – every bit of it.

I met Sue.

Fell in love.

Grew younger.

Found constancy.

Congruence.

Reference to bodies, space and time became the norm.

And time became relative.

Two atomic clocks, one left with Sue

Another fired in the rocket of my departure.

I travel muchly, fatigue myself phoning every five minutes

And doing little work and less anything else.

I return a day later and

Lo and behold: She has grown younger because she did not age

And I older by the hundred years of solitude experienced being away

from each other.

Or is it because she uses oil that fights the seven signs of ageing

Which are: the worry over ageing

The price of the cream

The fact that all the models advertising it are twelve

That an iron would not flatten my ageing wrinkles (ooops laughter lines

for I am a man – only women wrinkle)

… et cetera … et cetera …

That was exactly what that twit Albert meant: $E=MC^2$

Where E is our love

M is the time spent apart

C is the speed of missing each other

Squared because so agonising.

And through that I have also discovered the theory of everything:

The love each to each

Makes life a little peach

And aren't rhymes so bloody untrue

And not perfect like my little ---

Enough. This is revolting stuff. But is it not heaven itself to those truly

in love?

And physics makes two times in one so possible

So Palestine and Israel can also both be one…

Painting, 'Country Dream', by the poet.

Empty

When I consider how my life's become so empty

I sense the need to reinvent it with purpose.

What purpose?

The sun has set and all is dark and unknown.

All the past's meaningless so making this product so.

What does it mean now that books are anathema?

What avails it that our world's dumbed down

With gadgets, cretinous media and pernicious religion?

What does it matter that education's dead

And its intensive care is at the hospice

Parentless, alone and condemned to fail?

What is it to anyone that all that is left is a sense of loss

Worthlessness, heavy souled and destined to solitude?

What purpose indeed?

But reinvent it I will.

I know not what.

I know not how.

I know not where or when.

All I know is that there will be a new world

Triumphal, urged forth, willed on,

Marching alone "*to strive, to seek, to find*"

That bliss that is called creator's and - maybe - Creator's

And so leading to real peace.

Painting, 'Heat', by the poet.

Epiphany

Titum titum titum titum

Tumti tumti tumti tumti.

Tititum tititum tititum tititum.

Tumtiti tumtiti tumtiti tumtiti.

And thus was the year since September 09.

Changing its rhythm and travel speed.

It became a burden to an enfeebled soul.

Impossible to carry: noisy knotted and tired.

Each time one knot untied and another was newly wired.

And then, on that fateful morning of the sixth;

The house of cards came tumbling down,

Each card a gigantic stone ready to crush

An already fractured body and dispossessed mind.

Leaving a desert vast arid silent and ablaze.

Each grain of sand a question unanswered.

And with each grain a world of emptiness

In itself a desert vast arid silent and ablaze

With each grain of sand a world within a world.

And so on into a vast dark deep eternity.

Solace: Trees, flowers, Mozart, Beethoven,

Dickens, Tolstoy, Austen, Taha Hussein and al-*Qur'an*.

Maybe history in search of identity, but there;

Finding such cruelties, hypocrisies and bad faith.

Other disciplines from physics to mathematics

The $E=MC^2$ and the best of all framed:

Standing precariously by the window where stood

"No shit Sherlock?" and in the previous year;

"$N = R^* \times fp \times ne \times f1 \times fi \times fc \times L$".

So, there is life out there in the vast universe.

Comforting thought that there is another us

Somewhere and hopefully doing a lot better.

And all that confusion did nothing to improve,

Or alleviate to end suffering and happiness prove.

Sixty two years of exiled existence,

Occupation, murder, torture, oppression and

All in the name of a vindictive god

Called "just" in an abusive book of mythology.

Sixty two years of the Jewish "*Never again*".

Of "*We have the smell of Auschwitz and Treblinka*

In our nostrils - so world, never again."

And we, innocent victims of displacement,

Expulsion, rape, killing and dreams of home

Are told, "*You don't feel our pain.*

We are the Chosen People and you are a myth."

And we ask, "*When we lose our home,*

Do we not cry? When we lose our loved ones,

Do we not weep? When you stab us,

Do we not bleed? When you take our lands,

Do we not roam the earth wandering and

Do we not seek revenge, liberation and freedom?"

Rhetorical questions for which, as an exception,

The answer is, *"No! For you are terrorists."*

"We are not!" we reply. *"We fight for freedom.*

We fight for our homes, lands, orchards and

Memories spread over thousands of years."

This cruelty, inspired by a vindictive non existent god;

A prima donna throwing his weight about

Invented by vulnerable fools to justify

Their emptiness, cruelty and endless malice.

All became too much for us and the weight

Crushed our soul and drove a stake in our heart.

And so, on the sixth of September 2009,

We awoke and broke the blessed Sabbath rule

For we had a breakdown on a Sunday!

So, where, in that fairy tale, he rested on the seventh

We, living in the real world, crumbled and fell.

Closed all doors, burnt all bridges, sunk all ships

And withdrew into the safe abode of our books

Living quietly, occasionally deliberating with Christ.

Nights were disturbed with dreams awash with terror.

Days followed days connected each to each

By the one central question over arching all:

The theme soothes but the deeds are evil

And hurt our central core incomprehensibly.

It took a year to find a little answer to this quiz.

Elementary my dear Watson using deductive reasoning.

Simple really, myths are myths. Stories,

Intended by primitive man to explain a difficult world,

Like Greek myths so we can cope with suffering

If Pandora's box had its reasons and added a little hope

And so with the silly story of creation and all

Those children's tales that followed making some sense

Of what can not be explained away for complexity.

Till, that is, a morning fine, breezy and green

Standing in a forest looking over the fields

Eyes scanning from right to left undulations interminable;

A voice there came from the void and said:

"Blessed are the poor in spirit: for theirs is the kingdom of heaven…"

Laying out the simple truth that entered our soul

And told us what was right and what was not.

Closing the door on emptiness, cruelty and vacuity.

Painting, 'I Love You', by the poet.

Eternal Love

Early one morn I betook me on a long contemplative walk

To my favourite forest where even trees do occasionally talk.

I considered how this, like another, two hundred years ago

Walked by the lake reflecting on some grand scheme to go.

His was *The Prelude* much loved by me and hated by most.

Like his other with its ghastly dancing and waving daffodil host.

What to write and how and when and about whom.

The whom I knew and could see clearly.

That soft face with the pretty eyes looking at me.

The when too was easy, why, now of course.

How was a little more complex as was the what.

As I walked listening to chattering trees.

Another epic poem about love

That would blot out Shakespeare's Juliet and her Romeo

And Eloise and Abelard as well as Paul et Virginie

Such poetic prose on l'amour tout à fait éternel

Or even, oh most poetic of all,

Othello's story telling and Desdemona's tears

But not the green eyed monster that destroyed all.

And there, in the midst of the forest, she stood,

Stately in her eternal un-diminishable beauty;

And smiled at my struggles and

With her little finger motioned me to her;

Where in an embrace unfathomable we stayed

74

Until it became so apparent that the epic poem

Was like the moving finger that moved and once did write.

Our love is the eternal epic poem.

Otherwise words are meaningless and

Images futile,

For her eyes look into a new world;

Unparalleled forevermore.

And I retraced my steps back to where my epic poem lives

And loves.

Painting, 'Jerusalem', by the poet.

God's Little Acre

Dedicated to Professor Naom Chomsky recently elected the most

powerful intellect in the world and barred by Israel from entering God's

little acre, Palestine

Green run unending and circuitous sans fin

Each entwined with each so that no beginning there was

And no end will there be. Like Loving but not knowing.

Ever green greening evermore green run without

Shades greened from then till now and so full.

Ask the olive tree its secrets, it talks not but it can be heard

By those who have ears to hear and can be seen

By those who have eyes to see and can be felt

By those who have fingertips to feel.

Oh, pour out your heart, empty yourself of endless phrases.

Repeated run green run live run and full of familiarity.

Language is the womb of our intellect giving expression

To our real run realities Love like run into a woman's flesh.

Never ending although drying like green leaves

To die and be reborn and reborn run run run.

And so, green run and around until

Language roads take us there where all is perfection:

God's Little Acre. Green run and ever abiding.

Painting, 'Naïve Tree', by the poet.

God's Promise

May your God damn you for your murderous thoughts,

Your cruelty and your utterly sickening indifference

To our plight, our deaths, our injuries and our Diaspora.

As you sit in your comfortable homes on your free lands,

Let us have a thought falling alongside your biscuit crumbs

Made wet by dunking in your tea as we are dunked in blood

And overwhelming hatred for all that you call God's Will.

And when your child is born and you teach it the story of The Promise

And, how, that villain Muhammad stole Palestine,

Just for the sheer hell of it and just to annoy the real God,

And when you watch the Palestinian headless baby held up,

Now "*Eyeless in Gaza*" and then, when you turn to your delicious

Sunday dinner,

After your hypocritical prayers – give us a thought.

Just one thought.

Deny not your God.

Deny not His *Promise*.

Deny not your faith.

Just look at us and see that our redness

Is blood oozing from a cut not of us but borne by us,

That our tears are just salted homesickness

The kind you feel when on a short holiday,

Except ours is a permanent holiday.

Look at our dead piled up indifferently

In the name of your faith and belief.

Deny us not our pain and our hurt.

For, my friends, we are human like you.

Our tears are salted like yours but now more frequent.

Our blood is red like yours but now more on show.

Our souls once born free just like yours but now oppressed.

And our children born innocent just like yours but now filled with hate.

Our loves permanent just like yours but now cut short by a bullet.

Our homes precious just like yours but now lived in by others.

Our laughter welcome just like yours but now drowned in loss.

And our lives God given just like yours but now taken by others.

Keep all that you have and just

Give us some look of pity

For all we now have is pity

As our homeland and our security.

Meanwhile, keep pretending to yourselves

That your faith is about Love and Forgiveness

As long as the love is not of us

And the Forgiveness is all theirs for

Dispossessing us, murdering our loved ones

And taking our homes.

And continue to lecture us on *The Promise*.

As if we had no feelings

No life

No liberty

And no God.

May your God damn you for this cruelty.

Evermore a thorn in our heart and

A reminder of an injustice born out of your cruel fairy tales.

And may He forgive you your cruelty,

And us our enduring injustice.

Painting, 'Naked Paths through an Olive Grove', by the poet.

Hush! Hush! Hush!

Hush! Hush! Hush!

If there is a time when silence is apt;

It is now. Hush!

To worship The Lord?

No. Hush!

To mourn the dead then?

No. Hush!

To tend the sick and weary?

No. Hush!

Why then?

Why? To speak of love.

Hush! Hush! Hush!

If you speak of love then you hush not...

Hush! Hush! Hush!

Love needs not one word

Or noise to speak its name.

Maybe a look,

A smile,

A sigh,

A wave,

A raised eyebrow,

A kiss,

Any sign,

And Love roars its deafening silent sound.

Painting, 'Palestine', by the poet.

Morning

Mornings call out to my poetic soul to step outside

And by years of tradition daily and regularly abide.

To walk outside, look around and welcome the new day.

For years back this has been my classic daily way.

This morning was no different, as I stood by the ivy cascading down

the wall,

And stared at the sky working downwards listening to the call.

Aye, birds had started their matinal converse hours ago,

And I had heard them and, poet like, my inner voice went "*Lo!*"

For we of the Muse would anything do any time

To get a decent melodious little singing rhyme,

And so talk in tongues strange and foreign to abide

By the godly Muse and stay by her wording side.

"*Lo!*" Quoth I. "'*Tis the birds a-singing and time to prove,*

That life is beautiful and every living creature is on the move.

So, up betimes, down the apples and pears

Which sounds better than 'down the stairs'."

And I stood in the garden and wondered how even

Now, in my old age, this must be the Garden of Eden.

Green, silent, growing, alive and so full of Love.

Aye, there's the rub, for nothing suitably rhymes with Love.

Except, that is, Love. Marlowe tried to invite her to come,

Live with him and be his *Love*,

And that way that and this to "*prove*",

Which then rhymed but, alas, it does not so today.

It matters little, listener, for my words are magic.

To mesmerise you with so that you look

In my eyes and lie back and surrender to my soft kiss,

And hard manhood entering your loving portal.

Rhyme or no rhyme, the words of love,

In "*England's green and pleasant land*"

Make all music seem base and this

Our Love, is indeed music enough.

And so, you can say when you will

That indeed Love is powerful and still

In any language, believe in the truth:

'Tis true, that '*Amor vincit omnia*.'

Amor vincit omnia: Love conquers all.

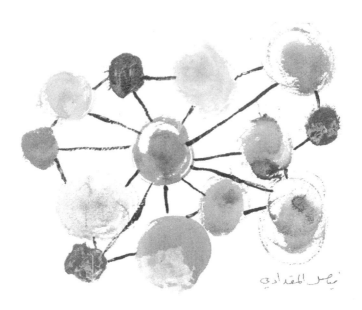

Painting, 'Peace Conference', by the poet.

Red Patch

Dreams are made of those fleeting thoughts that

Invade our busy solitude running onwards.

Dreams that refuse to face a reality so painful

That our running pace increases in inverse proportion

To its strength; or weakness as it should properly be.

Then, when the dream comes fleeting through

And the phone does not ring to kill it

And those around us do not scream or cry or

Play life's little games of failed aspirations;

Then the dream crawls outwards into the sleepless night

And invades the day's struggle wavering this way and that

Full of good intentions and loveless and alone;

Then some truths gently crawl and creep and

Show themselves: First rather comforting and

Beautiful: A little like the realisation that the long

Unpaid debt is but printed paper and so what.

And the cards that build our house are also made of paper

And those dreams, termite like, eat away invisibly

And the house of cards comes tumbling down

More loveless and alone.

I watched you die three years ago

And took away much relief when you did

For your agony sickened me and frightened the

Other me sitting in the armchair thinking

On what it all meant.

I thought of the things you said

Always tongue in cheek as if the

Seriousness of saying '*I love you and I care*'

Were a rope wound around your neck

While you stood on the edge of a chair

Fearful of the inevitable fall.

You said much that made sense and angered me.

Three years later you and those truths

Have become little dreams that crawl and creep

And bring my little house of cards down

Leaving me alone and loveless and without

A oneness that I strove for and killed you for.

Sky, rain down red sand on the red

Red patch where my brother lies.

Rain down red red sand like drops of

Blood on Canaan land turning wine into water

And all our yesterdays into a vast, empty, void

A nothing to play in and dream in and wake up in.

Rain red sand on all our dreams

And all those reddening cards that made a flimsy house.

The red patch is so small that

If you look from the end of the

Universe you will not see it

Just as you do not see it

When you stand on it

Staring into the clumsy ugly

Hole - eternal home for now.

And the universe is so huge

It has no beginning and no end

And neither does my lonely lovelessness

And its ugly house of cards.

Rain. Rain. Rain.

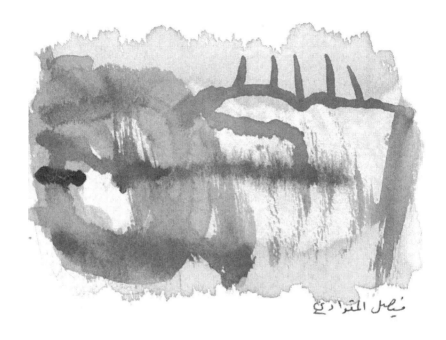

Painting, 'Refugee', by the poet.

Scum

He put his cigarette out in the cup of coffee,

Sipped the ash off his tray

And didn't know the difference.

Eyebrows thickened and cheekbones aching

He clutched his soul to protect it.

To fend off a vapid vacuous vampire

That sucked his life out of its shell.

Squeezing hard and frantically furrowing

Until, semi-conscious, he ejaculated life

That died instantly in the middle of

Fitful sleep eyes wide open and aching.

Fuck this mortal world for the pain it gives us.

Fuck this life for all the hurt it doles out.

Your loved ones fuck you up in the name

Of caring, loving and needing.

Insinuating their emotions wormlike into

Your veins until your blood dries out

And they go off to fuck up someone else.

Vicious, nasty, unloving like a dried cunt

Scratching against the shaft until it, too, bleeds.

I would rather sell my arse to a stranger

Than whore my soul to my loved ones.

Ungrateful wretches: too self-centred

To sense the hell we've entered…

... and call it Palestine.

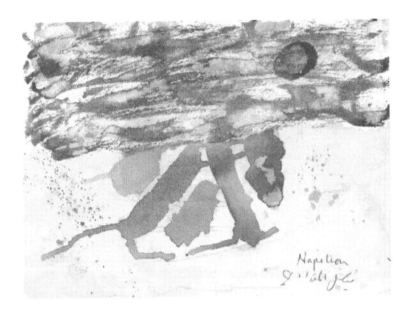

Painting, 'Napoleon', by the poet.

So Long

"*Those are pearls that were his eyes*"

That sad half demented Phoenician.

A very long, long time ago, when,

All felt cold cloud full and sunless

Those eyes sprung endless crystalline

Tears wherein were washed times,

Acceptances rejected and fears dreamed

A thousand times and a thousand deaths.

Tear by tear lived a moment, hesitated,

Then dropped, rolling away from its source.

A fractured soul twisting invisibility

And each little, rolling, warm, saline

Tear dented fractured incomplete souls.

And then?

And then?

If you have eyes to see

If you have a heart to feel

If you have a hand to hold

If you have life to breathe

If you have a soul to share:

Then see, feel, hold, start breathing life

And share from time immemorial

Till the dawn of death starts it

All again, in this and many other lines.

Let not those pearls reflect sadness.

Let not these pearls contain a world

Left friendless, soulless and alone.

Let not these pearls roll away

Leaving an empty ache.

Let each look be that of love;

Each tear that of joy and hope,

For this is the real thing.

And when I am old and sun setting away

Thinking how Palestine was no more and now is,

And how England was and now is no more,

That all is done

Newly born now have the field

And to Paris often departicularised

Returning as if from a gentle walk.

'Oh darling, I can not hold it anymore,

Let me. Let me. Let me fill you with my love.'

And then, and only then, did their eyes meet

And love flooded the earth and all was sweet.

When I am old and mumbling away

Words that no one understands

Or cares to understand

And the whooshing in the brain

Speaks of a life gone by

Relief soon at hand.

My son my father,

My daughter a kindly mother

Caring for old time's sake

And all the memorable laughter reverberating forever more.

When all that and much much more

Happens

Because it will do

As certain as eyes that shut

When a gentle kiss is cut.

When the end is almost upon me

Welcomed with a smiling tremble.

Then I want to know

That all our life was full

To the brim and all our

Tomorrows repeated our yesterdays,

I want to say a gentle prayer

In one word

Insistent

Interminable

Joyful loving loved

Her name that only she knew.

"What did he say?"

"Oh nothing, he is hallucinating, poor fellow…"

"I thought he said 'let me, let me, let me lose, lose, lose, or something

like that…"

"No. You're hearing things."

But then only you and I will know what I did say my love.

So come. Put your hand in mine

And let us go forward leaving so much behind

And let not anyone even think that ours was just a little event

Soon to be forgotten like so much else.

Painting, 'Neuchâtel', by the poet.

The Epic

Looking out of the patio doors as darkness descended,

I discerned colours darkening their hue day's lightened.

It occurred to me how each day creeps by,

With the same unanswerable question 'Why?'.

The brain fevered with notions, thoughts, ideas assuaged,

Seeking expression but silenced by life's passage.

Like Wordsworth's ardent desire to write it;

What the 'it' was or is into no niche does it fit.

A work to explain man's ways to God

As Milton tried showing God's way to man.

How Adam and Eve were blessed, disobeyed and so fell

And how all the ills were born to visit all beyond

Until His spilt blood into endless drops

Each and every one to salve our mortal sins.

That same epic, God born, to come down to this,

My mortal eyes admiring this land full of consequent bliss.

Once the darkness has fallen, I look out and see

Silhouetted trees waving their arms in supplication to be

Given another night's life with endless memories

Of happy summer days reading in their shade.

And that epic suddenly reveals itself in glory.

Every detail, every little insignificant point,

Ulysses like, through Dublin's streets following Bloom

Through the trivia his and Molly's life full of doom

This epic will be cast in its natural colours

Born of Love friendship and a giant creative urge.

Painting, 'Ghosts', by the poet.

The Forest

I heard the Devil speak earnestly by my left ear

The pain in his voice full of hatred, bitterness and fear.

"*Thinkst thou,*" quoth he. "*Thinkest thou that I, who had seen the face*

of God, am not tormented by ten thousand hells in being deprived of it

forevermore. Why, this is Hell nor am I out of it."

This, as is often my wont, set me thinking of grander things than daily
toil.

If knowing Him be bliss, so not be but its empty and meaningless foil.

If the forest where I stood is all in all for all who ought to see,

And, if standing under His wondrous creations makes me know how to
be.

Then, Mephestopheles is right with his ten thousand torments.

I walked on, pensive with a mind full of woes, wonders and haste.

Trying hard to calm it, this wondrous world not to waste.

For, of late, we have rushed, ran, roved and removed remorselessly

In preparation for empty events "*full of sound and fury,*

Signifying nothing". A tale "*told by an idiot*" dribbling words meaning
naught.

Then I saw a tree. A giant alive. It stood majestically and stared at me.

An insignificant little being staring up in wonder. Looking for all I can
see.

What is this tree thinking of? How long has it stood here? What has it
seen?

A thousand years. More. And I, with my three score and ten, just been

Thinking myself complex, knowledgeable and full of thought.

I, not a handful of the tree's inner rings but still regarding me

As infinitely superior and in His image created to toil, seek, strive and

know.

But then, my tree smiled at me and, arms outstretched to the sky

Moving, waving and imploring for they knew not what, spake these

words.

"Do not compare your years to mine. Yes I have seen much and for

long.

I have had lovers beyond number fumble their clumsy Love beneath

my boughs.

I have watched each doing the same and looking as one, for naked,

we change not.

I have only seen fashion change over hundreds of years.

And I have lived longer than you and seen more secrets than your

brain could carry.

But..." Said my aged tree at last, with eyes bright and heart so light.

"I have not tasted the Love that you have. Felt her softness. Heard her

words.

I have not tasted her gentle kiss and felt her innocent hand on my very

life

Urging me to show her how I loved her and then cup her heart in mine.

So, you see, your three score and ten are, with that love, an eternity.

For love has no time. No end. No circumference. It is, just. It is as it is.

It is."

And I walked back home so happy and full of life.

To write those few words without any strife.

To send to her today of all days

When He rose to be with us always.

Painting, 'Happy New Year', by the poet.

The Realpolitik of the PLO's 14.12.88 Declaration

Forty years by three hundred and sixty five with leap extras by twenty

four by sixty by sixty.

Each second dripping burning acid.

Thousands killed many more killing.

Millions displaced.

A hundred million in fear.

Then some stone thrown politically

A few tyres burnt judiciously.

Peace. Violence renounced.

Rights recognised. All's well.

Such is politick.

The politics of those who died

For political ends.

Politics. They live on.

A move most politicque.

Those who died and those suffered and suffer ask:

What are politics?

Where's my bread?

Where's my home?

What's all this?

Have I slept for forty years?

Oh! Oh! What an awful nightmare.

What is realpolitik please?

Let's go home. We never left.

'Jerusalem in Winter', Library of Congress,

http://www.loc.gov/pictures/item/mpc2004004034/pp/

Telephone

'Allo?

Hello!

Ah I've got a line at last

Out of this ravaged death land.

How are you? The children?

You wife? What're you doing?

Celebrating Christmas. Opening presents.

What about you?

The same. But we have fireworks.

Bright. Smokey. Noisy.

With every crackle another X-mas

Gone. Flashing against wintering skies.

Jesus is born today and the sky is full bright.

Whirls. Falls. Shudders. And dies.

Who says X-mas is no longer grand

In Beirut. Lebanon. Holiest land.

Well I must go now. Your old

Dad is here. Love to the children.

And love to you too my poor

Poor.

Sister.

Poor. Poor. Ravaged. Deathland.

Goodbye.

And oh yes – Merry Christmas.

What's the weather like?

Say hello ....

'Palestinian Refugee Camp', www.al-awda.org/camps.html

Refugee Camp

"God! That photograph of the Palestinian Camp looks Biblical.

Almost apocalyptic. Heart breaking. But it does show

That God's hand is in all of this.

Theirs is the Promised Land and the Palestinians

Are Muslim invaders who should move on.

112

Ah! The Lord is so wise, so gentle, so just

And so jealous… Amazing…"

And she crossed herself several times as she handed back

The photograph

Containing a tent city

Under that jealous God's angry dark clouds

Covering endless Muslims who are hell bent on destroying

Jews and Christians (who, in Israel, are not Arabs really…)

"Muslims are fake," she added, smiling lovingly. *"Like a fake five Dollar*

bill. It almost takes you in… but then you look and you know better.

Only the Lord is real… all else is fake…" and her big eyes twinkle -

Affectionately at the Palestinian friend's face -

Little seeing the deep hurt of his lacerated heart and home

That fake refugee bastard seeking redress for his people's sins…

down a dark hot still alleyway

steps crunching forward

a knock loud and dark

like a grandfather clock passing time

i have come are you ready

steps upwards left another knock

thundering

birds twittering for time

down a dark hot windstilled alleyway

questions fly hard territorial words

who am i where are we

the only reply from mass graves with

plenty of time

'Street scene near the Jaffa Gate in Jerusalem', Palestine, Library of Congress,

http://www.loc.gov/pictures/item/mpc2004007051/pp

This poem, originally with the title 'Watching War on TV', was first published by Anchor Books: Foskett, David (Editor), *TV Memories*, 1996, ISBN 1 85930 380 3 (hardback) and 1 85930 385 4 (paperback).

Watching War on the Diaspora TV

Rumbling distanced glowed alight.

Across a grey horizon houses craggy and spotlighted.

Flare after flare.

The prospect seemed pleasing to the camera eye

As it blinded frame after frame

Of a city burning.

Strange how it rumbled but didn't blow.

Strange how it lit up but didn't burn.

And the television screen vibrated.

There were no humans anywhere.

Humans don't live in this.

Do they?

'Femme de Ramallah', http://imad.mouaid.online.fr/pa/24.htm

This poem, originally with the title 'Wog', was first published by Anchor Books: Foskett, David (Editor), *Poets in Protest*, 1996, ISBN 1 85930 301 3 (hardback) and 1 85930 306 4 (paperback).

Palestinian in London

Wog!

Wog!

I hate you!

Stop it. Peace. I beg for peace.

No my friend don't defend me

For I fear it – your defence.

It's like lava flowing flowing.

Water it and it hardens like rock.

Even cities carved from rock die once.

But actions day by day word for word

Never writ never uttered

Always carve names on

Hearts

Spirits

and the else future

Like a cell faceless eyeless –

It multiplies and fills a million worlds.

Why, like you and I.

You and I.

> *This is only blank because we make it so.*

'Blank Frame' by the Poet.

This poem was first published by The *London Progressive Journal*, Saturday 3 November 2012.

Bahrain

History replays itself over and over again. An endless loop. And we watch. Mesmerised. As if it were the first time. And we never learn.

Do you remember the Hungarian Uprising? A fleeting moment of freedom crushed by Soviet tanks. And the Prague Spring? We danced for joy till the tanks arrived in Wenceslas Square.

Today is Bahrain's early Spring Revolution. The riot police opened fire at crowds entering the square this afternoon after the army withdrew. Suddenly the riot police also withdrew.

The crowds are dancing in the square as I write. When will the tanks arrive?

Dance. Dance. Your freedom lives for a few minutes.

And three refrigerated lorries with Saudi Arabian number plates full of dead demonstrators were last seen driving over the highway to Saudi Arabia. An American filmed them loading the bodies. He has now disappeared.

I wish that I could wrench my Arab soul out of my body and replace it with something less painful. More loving.

I would replace it with my Palestinian soul but that has been arrested by the Israeli security forces for being peaceful. "*Non violent terrorism*" was the charge.

Let us sit in a circle and tell stories of times gone by and times to come. Of Arab glory and Western shame. Of promises crushed and of kings' lies and revolutions gone by.

Till the tanks arrive. And by tonight, those dancing now will lie still. Some dead. Others pretending to be. And most? Well, they died a long time ago. When they were born Arabs.

History replays itself over and over again. An endless loop. And we watch. Mesmerised. As if it were the first time. And we never learn.

'Little Sisyphus', Old City Jerusalem, Palestine,

www.palestinespeaks.wordpress.com/the-future-of-palestine

BP and the American Dream

"*Mr. Chairman?*" asked the Congressman in a light suit.

"*Mr. Chairman, has anyone been fired for this disaster?*"

Mr. Chairman, being British and a master in the art of prevarication,

Looked a little hurt and replied that an investigation will determine

culpability.

The Congressman was not happy because Americans had died

And Americans had lost revenue and Americans had paid the price

For BP's greed taught at the Harvard School of Business.

"*Mr. Congressman*?" should have asked the Chairman.

"*Has anyone been fired for the death of tens of thousands of Iraqis?*"

"*Has anyone been fired for the death of thousands of Afghans?*"

"*Mr. Congressman, has anyone been fired for the daily murder of*

Palestinians?"

"*Has anyone been fired for the killing of a whole nation?*"

"*Mr. Congressman, has anyone been fired for your country's moral*

cowardice?"

"*That moral cowardice that sanctions Israel's genocide of a whole*

nation?"

"*Mr. Congressman, has anyone been fired for your hypocrisy?*"

"*Fired for your double standards?*"

"*Mr. Congressman, you taught us free market business*

And our profit on it is that we can cheat, steal and deceive, Mr.

Congressman."

Thank you BP for showing the Americans for what they are:

Self engrossed, greedy, deceitful, dishonest and politically bankrupt

Like you will soon be, Mr. Chairman.

And then your American dream will become your nightmare

As it has been ours since those heady dreams of 1776

Were turned on their heads

To make the founding fathers their legacy of dreads.

'Palestinian old man by an almond tree in blossom', Library of Congress,

http://www.loc.gov/pictures/resource/matpc.02471/

Happy Birthday Mr President

On hearing that President Shimon Peres, President of Israel and

Peace Laureate, secretly writes poetry and has just had some of it put

to music to celebrate his 86th birthday.

Happy birthday to you

Happy birthday to you

Happy birthday mithter prethident

Happy birthday to you.

Many happy returns Mr President.

You will excuse my little joke Mr President

For I'm no Marilyn Monroe and you are no John F Kennedy.

But we do have a few things in common:

Both hypocrites we, both liars, both cheats.

I because I still live when Palestine has died

Murdered by you and your chosen people;

And you for aiding and abetting in the crime

And getting the Nobel Peace Prize for your efforts.

You share the godlike pantheon

With such low life as Sadat, Arafat and others.

But, Mr President, we have another thing in common.

We are both word smiths mesmerising a trusting public

As God does with his words except He tells truths

Which we then mangle to our little designs.

Tell me, Mr President, when the much lamented Rabin told your

soldiers

Their arms to break and when,

That night, a passer by filmed the Purity of Arms

Lay three Palestinians on three rocks

And, using other rocks, crack their arms,

I say, Mr President, was that the night you wrote

"*Israel be not sad*"?

Were these rocks, that smashed their bones,

The same rocks that supported Christ's bloody feet?

Or maybe that held him high to give his Sermon?

Were these rocks sacred to Islam for pointing the way

Or to Jews for providing the Jerusalem stones

To build The Temple that holds our national woes?

Mr President, I have a small piece of land

Not far from that Golden beach where they sang your words.

It has red soil that smells of my father's sweat and mother's birth

waters

When she brought me forth to replenish Palestine.

Mr President, the soil has grains innumerable,

Each a little world with a million little people

Like you and I, wandering in sadness.

Mr President, I will share the grains with you

For I, too, have become a wandering Jew

Waiting to go home to Jerusalem

To exchange a salam aleikem

With my brother Christians and Jews.

What do you say Mr President.

Share and share alike?

Mr President?

Mr President?

Are you there Mr President?

Look after my grains for me Mr President.

Happy Birthday Mr President.

'Old Map of Palestine', 1833,

www.davidrumsey.com/search?utf8=√&term=Palestine

The History Lesson

"*Good morning! Good morning!*" Good morning!

Not the bloody general again

Study pack up there and back

That "*cheery old card*" who "*did for 'em*" all

The fat fascist fumbling swine.

Good morning! Today the defeat of Germany

Tomorrow the defeat of Germany.

Next week the Bible (mine not yours)

Where Christianity and wars don't mix

Though we can change that you know.

"*Good morning! Good morning!*" Good morning!

A seven minute test on Neuilly, Trianon,

Sèvres and trillions of Marks for a new loaf.

Field Marshal Hindenberg gave Hitler tea

Before he lost his brained penis to a niece.

Good morning! Use the map to help you.

You know where you're going with a map

Uphill to the Western Front romantically

Sculptured contributory with sponged blood

In glory and power beyond whimperings.

"*Good morning! Good morning!*" Good morning!

Let's melt all guns all deaths in pain

And make a kettle, a cup and a smile

Use the trenches to grow food and flowers

And make history a really nice novel.

'Virgin and Child with St. Joseph', French artist unknown, *Book of Hours*, Use of Tours, c. 1490-1500. BL MS Harley 2877 f.18v.

Tomorrow

How did you know all the way around this world in that land where you tell me that you swim, read, swim some more, make love, read and then discuss.

How did you know that dad was upset that Monday night?

God blight this world

For making our tomorrow shrouded

In an irretrievable past;

Laid low by hedging and fencing.

Yet our tomorrows will soon come

And pass joining invisible joints

To that abusive and merciless past.

But then, there is the game:

That fucking game our parents so loved to play

Our husbands, wives and all our loves

As yours will never do, my friend.

Enjoy the moment for itself

And you'll vanquish the past,

Future, and even, one day, death itself.

Then, this world need not be blighted

Since it's yours as night follows day – my loving son.

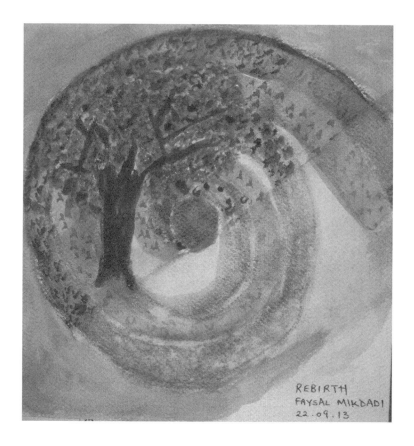

Painting, 'Rebirth', by the poet.

Miracle at Cana

"Our Father who art in Heaven"

Pray with me for those gone to Thy Mercy.

Their blood, Lord, washed their innocence away.

They were Canaanite each and every one.

"*Thy will be done*".

It was, they say, a tragic mistake

That hallowed the soil with a red hued lake

And took them to "*Thy Kingdom come*".

No longer do they need their daily bread

No others' sins forgiven in their debt.

No longer temptation into which be led

Or apologies for mistakes oft repeated once said.

Lord, they were wretchedly poor

Wishing to live as their forebears did

Quietly toiling their turf in anonymity hid

Until the '*Grapes of Wrath*'

Every grape a skull

Every juice a cup of blood overflowing.

Lord, You remember turning water into wine

At that wedding in Cana?

The wedding bore fruits

That toiled the land

That bore more souls

Who died this day.

One miracle too many, my Lord,

That impresses the faithless horde.

Water, wine, grapes and blood

Backwards forwards in Cana

Those red children: who could look?

Their very sleeping innocence a holy book.

Lord, where You there at Cana?

A child was there who took to sleep.

Where You that child at Cana, Lord?

Did you see, through that child's misted eyes

How they mocked your fare?

Did You, heart overflown, curse and go?

Come back, then, Lord, and heal the Canaanite's child.

And turn the red red soil

Back to its gentle flowing water

Wherein the child to swim, splash, laugh and –

And die an old old being without gun's flame

Having lived, toiled, loved while whispering You Name.

For, you see, 'tis best to be forgot

For being a poor little sot

Than be forgot in human cruelty

For having died seeking sanctuary.

Essex cottage where the poet lived 1975-1989. Photographed by the poet.

And to England I – September 19, 1987

After a long and quiet walk I returned home

Leaving my thoughts behind

On the marshes and the fields.

Thoughts of twenty years of British life

Twenty years of England my own village.

Twenty years.

So much has happened and will.

Twenty years.

Am I an exile? A citizen?

What does England mean.

In truth now.

In truth?

It is difficult to tell.

Still romancing after twenty years:

of Dickens and Scott, of Shakespeare

Hornby trains and plastic planes

terraced doll's house.

Twenty years and still everlastingly romancing.

But in truth? The reality of England?

Do not romance any more. There must be things you.....

Not hate – can't say that. Too strong a word.

Must be things not quite right?

Come. In truth.

Thatcher? But I like her and love to hate her.

Baker? But I hate him and hate to like him.

The Church? It does me no harm. In fact I like the bazaars.

Education? I teach. Worse luck.

Norman Tibbit? Let's not get carried away. England I love.

There are limits.

Say to me in truth what do you love so?

I talk to you imaginary and no one bothers me.

I walk with a hole in my sock and so what.

I do not visit and do not receive.

I am harmless and so uncertified.

This is the real England

Where alone a person can still stand

Else he would fall

And have his face trodden into the sand.

In Britain – there are no eccentrics

Just persons.

In truth you're still romancing.

You really are.

I do see some minor changes a few petty laws...

Aha! In truth.

But it is England –

The romancing land

In truth.

And home I walked leaving imaginary friends behind.

Happy anniversary daddy.

I hope that you have another twenty years as successful as the last.

Your loving and ever faithful little girl.

I hope the next twenty years in England have been happy.

Love Richard aged eight.

To my husband: You came you saw you conquered.

I'm so glad you did.

Here's to the next twenty years.

I will never desert Mr. Micawber and Palestine be damned

And Israel blessed for expelling you to my arms.

This is England. Where I'm loved.

All this and so much more.

'Women from Ramallah in Palestine', Library of Congress,

http://www.loc.gov/pictures/item/2005686950/

The Wall

There is a whole new world behind yonder wall,

Standing so imperious, immovable and tall.

It is a world of beauty, silence and peace.

Standing this side, all is noise and sad toil,

People full of misery, memories and tempers fit to boil.

Ours is a world of sheer ugliness and hurts.

I so dearly wanted to go beyond that wall,

And see divine beauty making all sadness pall.

To leave this life behind and live it no more.

But mine was living this side forevermore,

And seeing the green green world nevermore.

All my tears would not cleanse my world of its cruelty.

I, a heathen of yore, knelt and prayed for long,

For a chance to cross over to that land of love so strong.

And prayed again and again for so long.

Suddenly a little door opened and I ran through

To the brave new world with greenery and life anew.

Wonder of all wonders was what I found.

A new world just like my old with a man like me

Intoning about the whole new world for me to see

Behind the tall wall where he stood so forlorn.

And I heard an inner voice whispering to the few,

"It's all the same, for the world is in you."

In this new world either side of this tall wall.

Painting of the poet in the mid-1980s painted by Dave Martin and gifted to the poet on his fortieth birthday.

The Child Is Father of the Man

Early morning darkness merged into sleepy dreams.

It was a special day of going shooting with father.

New gun gleaming and well polished smelt of oil.

Its one small nozzle a contrast to father's double barrelled shotgun.

But it might have been a howitzer to my little eyes.

Father's car always smelt clean, its leather seats shining bright.

I sat beside his giant body with massive hands gripping the wheel.

I wanted to go back to sleep but feared losing the moment.

Father's taciturn silence awed me so I held my peace

And stared into the darkness giving way to a distant dawn.

The city receded and hills slowly emerged like giants

With distinguishable features staring back at me.

As each hill was climbed a bigger appeared to replace it,

And so more and more faces mocked my little world

With their vast expanse and lightening colours.

Atop the highest mountain the cold air stirred,

With father throwing a blanket over me and saying

"*Sleep on. Sleep on. I will wake you up on arrival,*"

I wanted manfully to declare that I had not been sleeping

And, as fellow hunter, I, too welcomed the cold dawn.

But I refrained for fear of appearing disobedient

And shut fast my eyes to please my father whose God like

Force was my domain, world and expanse of emerging

consciousness.

I pretended to sleep whilst staring out of the window

Observing every crag and every stone by the road.

I loved the trees most and knew some by name from previous trips.

These trees danced and flailed their arms about

And many stretched their long arms to the heavens

And seemed to pray fervently the way that I did under the pine tree

As my teacher did things to me that hurt me so

As he ordered me to stretch my arms up and I prayed for release.

I looked around at my father and saw his handsome face lit up

With full daylight now and his strong jaw covered in minute dark holes

I so loved to feel against my cheek when he kissed me good night

As I pretended to sleep to make the moment of rare love linger.

"*Beqa'a Valley*," announced my father with joy in his voice.

At a great distance I could just discern Baalbeck

Which always filled me with awe and fear even in pictures

Because of that painting in my history book of terrified people

Running as the earthquake struck and destroyed the sun city.

I used to stare at it for hours discerning every line of terror.

My teacher had seen me and invited me to look at other pictures

And then did those painful things to me so many times.

I remember asking father if that was how men made babies.

He had been driving and suddenly stopped the car by the beach

And asked where I had heard such things in a stern voice.

I lied and said at school where older boys told us

And, to my relief, he laughed and said that babies were not made like

that

And he explained and I was even more confused

But relieved not to be carrying my teacher's baby.

On the vast plains by the Roman ruins we breakfasted

On olives, fresh bread and a hot drink and I felt awfully grown up.

We packed the food away, locked the car and moved on

Holding our guns nozzle down like true hunters.

My father's shooting was as accurate as mine was futile.

I feared his disapproval and tried so hard and shot nothing but air.

As he gathered bird after bird he was beginning to get impatient with

me.

He quietly pointed out a bird and motioned for me to shoot it.

I took aim, sat its little head in my little sight and fired.

The bird fluttered and jumped about though not gleefully as I thought.

Father slapped me on my back and said well done!

I walked towards the writhing jumping bird reloading my gun.

I reached it and it looked up at me with those dumb eyes

Full of questioning as to why its perfect life was ending thus.

"Sorry", I whispered as my father called out to wring its neck.

I picked it up and it was warm with its head tilted quizzically

And eyes still staring reproachfully at me as I stared back.

Its wing was hanging uselessly by its side and I stroked its head.

I crouched down and put it on the floor and took out my tube of balm

An antiseptic father made me carry in case I cut myself.

I applied a generous dollop of cream to its wing

And shooed it off as quietly as I could adding aloud

"*It has flown off Baba. Flown off.*" In a voice pretending sorrow.

The bird still looked up at me as I, and it, slowly were obscured by a

huge shadow.

Father stood beside me and looked reproachfully.

He picked the bird up and quickly wrung its neck and threw it in the

pouch by his side.

"*It is kinder thus, my boy,*" said he quietly as he towered over me.

I slowly stood up, looked up at him and threw my gun on the ground.

His eyes caught mine as my vision exploded in streaming tears

And my body heaved with rising sobs and I saw my teacher

Holding me by my hair and grunting as I cried.

Father's face softened and he held his arms out

Encompassing my weeping frame and patting my head.

"*It was too early. Too early*," said he to other hunters gathering around

To witness this drama unfold of a hunter's son who could not kill.

One remarked that with such girlish sensitivity we were never going to regain

Palestine and my father looked annoyed and glowered at him.

Father picked the gun up and steered me towards the car

And as we walked he pointed out the trees and named some

And I named others as my tears dried and my sobbing subsided.

He threw both his gun and mine in the boot of the car.

We sat in the car and I said that I was sorry and begged he would not tell my sister

Because she might think me a little girl and he laughed

Patting my cheek several times and naming another tree.

The Eucalyptus that stretched so far up in the sky

That I could not make its top and I wondered if atop it lay

That place where all was peace and happy loving delay

Of any pain and fear and other such feelings as mine

In that place that everyone talked about so much and called Palestine.

Father drove us back slowly with many stops and laughs and much fun

And since then I never saw it again - or indeed any other such gun.

'Return to Sender', Jacek R. Kowalski, 1979,

www.palestineposterproject.org/artist/jacek-r-kowalski

Vietnam

It appeared so simple, yet impossible, then

As thousands were left standing speechless,

The wide-eyed betrayal awaiting re-education.

The Vietnam War was over, and the domino,

Still stood again topping the two million dead.

Simple; because we knew we were wrong.

Impossible; because we did little but live

Whilst others died, fed on it and died again.

Betrayal became a way of life with

Whooshing helicopter blades severing our arteries.

Twenty five years on, give or take a year

For these, like the dead, are mere statistics,

In Dorchester town, sat two.

She, no more than a child when Saigon fell

And he: maybe a questioning adolescent.

They sat: so much in love. More lovéd.

Talking.

Twenty five years on: all arteries now severed,

Blood well drained, leavening white skeletal lovers

Without function, junk fed and junk cultured.

But in love. Planning a wedding.

The white dress mattered more than

Those solemn vows.

The guest list fluctuated more

Than their combined passions.

Their wedding fare discussed,

Then discussed again and digested,

Those air full of trivial words: I love you.

shallow

empty

crass

so disjointed

dysfunctional

fashion freaked

prices well known and values ignored

passive

foolish

laughing at contented talk

Much, much more than died in Vietnam

Saigon that April day as I cooked a fillet steak in a red kitchen

And shed a tear for my friends

And a truly "*Shakespeherean Rag*" was born that day:

Meaningless, insubstantial and insecure.

Still:

I prefer the bleeding bleating modern fools in love

to the gaping bleeding open wounds:

war's only tool.

For it is said, with much truth,

That love does conquer all.

It conquered me

On Saturday evening in a small kitchen

Where colours exploded and blinded me to all else.

Keys on Palestinian embroidered cushion cover, photographed by the poet.

Waiting

I died and reached them pearly gates.

I am now British so I thought it polite to stand by and wait.

Men, women and children came and came.

I recognised a few over the first handful of years.

My wives, then daughter, son and their children.

They didn't recognise me because I sat quietly on a wooden bench.

I called out once but no voice there came.

A thousand years went by and I waited to be invited.

Another thousand years or so went by.

And I thought it not unreasonable to seek advice.

Advice from a man by the gate.

"*Peter?*" Asked I very quietly.

"*Aye, my son,*" he softly replied.

"*I have been watching you these two or so thousand years.*"

"*Thank you, sir,*" I replied. "*I had thought me become invisible.*"

"*No, my son, I can see you - clear and clear through you.*"

He looked at me and smiled so kindly that I gathered courage,

The courage to ask what I had to do to gain entry through the gates.

"*Why, my boy. Is that what you have been waiting for?*

Two thousand years waiting patiently.

No need my boy. You could have entered on day one."

"*But I did not know that I could, sir,*" faltered I.

"*Bless you, my son, I can see in your heart a Jerusalem and therein*

Resides Jesus after gaining entry all that time ago.

That and only that is all you need to go through."

And I walked in through these heavenly gates.

Never too late whatever the length I had to wait.

'The Old Mosque at Tiberias in Palestine', circa 1900-1920,

www.documentarist.com/the-old-mosque-at-tiberias-palestine-1900-1920

Whispering Trees

Whispering trees, what do you say, so quietly, every time I pass by?

Your branches waving and dancing in the breeze up so high?

What words speak you and on what subjects so secret and dark

Straining in this strong wind from side to side cracking your bark.

I often wonder by, thinking of things that have been and are still to be,

And I heard you talking loudly and really wanted to know what you

see.

For example, can you see into the future or do you know the past?

Do answer me and let me know before more life goes by so fast.

And, as I turned to retrace my steps home, I heard a voice speak,

And I turned around in terror for no person could I see for all I did

seek.

"It is I, my friend, your friend, the tree, wishing to give you what I can

About all that you appear to seek and can not find despite best laid

schemes.

I look far and wide seeing all that your race can not see,

And knowing all that has been, is and eventually will be.

I see a little girl by the name of Isabella Emma running free

In a golden field with you running after her happily in a loud spree.

You catch her and her squealed delight, throw her up and laugh aloud,

Then twirl her around and run homeward with your footsteps apt and

proud.

By a gleaming cottage stands a beauteous angel with a face like

Ashtaruth,

Waiting for you and Isabella and rewarding you with a smile full of

truth.

I see the three holding each to each and standing in a group,

And walking into the cottage in line laughing at being an army troupe.

A cottage so full of happiness, Love and such eternal ways,

In the Lord's hands protecting you and giving you happy days."

And so spoke my friends the trees telling all about I needed to do,

In order to make all perfect and build a life so just, happy and true.

And I walked back to my home sitting by those whispering trees,

And fell abed feeling safe, happy and certain of drinking life to the lees.

'Palestinians fleeing from Palestine', imeu.net

Words

We are the people of the word.

We are the people of the word.

Our words merge one into the other

Until we build a new world,

Fantastical and real.

That is how we enter the secret garden,

Smell its flowers,

Feel the dew,

Breathe in our little oneness

But still see the old desert

Through the rusty grill.

We are the people of the Word.

We weave our fantasies

Willingly and with choice.

Then we inhabit them.

Do you remember when you once said to me,

At the dawn of our lives and deaths,

You said, so long ago that it was only yesterday,

But here, time covers whole lives and expansive imaginings, my love,

You said,

"Your words mean so much to me

Your life means so much to me

And I will make yesterday tomorrow's history

And tomorrow yesterday's gentle balm

By loving all the sorrow out of you

And making up for those hurts that you so little deserved

My love

My five year old child

My twenty five year old man

My forty year old friend

My sixty year old husband."

And, amidst the gentle tears that streamed

Gleaming so softly in the night light

I could see so much.

And so far.

My wife left me to escape these very words

Flooding her life with a deadly torment.

I left my second wife because she drowned my words

In alcoholic abuse and I could no longer breathe.

Those words, said the first, where is the heart in them?

And the second, well, she asked, what the words did

Apart from create kindly escapes.

And I vowed never to build houses with words.

They abuse my little softer lives.

Now, my dear friend, I've got to the place.

I've found the eternal word.

With a colourful world in it

Perfect, clean, soulful, a whole life to span

She too, half a soul, the other half me – my little one.

Oh, I will rave and weave more little words

Spending the passion of the hour

Spanned to the next.

I will give and weave.

Weaving, weaving, weaving

Hamlet like: "*words, words, words*"

And she'll smile, hold my little face in her gentle hands,

Look me deeply in the eyes and say

'*Yes, my love. It is all right. You are loved for what you are.*

You have my permission, my darling'.

And not one word would she miss

With a hug, a smile and kiss.

D I Y Dee Eye Why D I Y

Oh, my eye

I have words to weave

Isn't it time to leave?

For I love you so; I begin again,

To love even me, and my words, through you.

'Type de jeune femme de Bethleem', unknown artist, License type: Editorial Royalty-free.

Lebanon Inchoate

Working as a wise, knowledgeable and deep sage

I opened my old *Thorndike* and traced down the page.

This wonderful book with my name as a school boy

Had become a favourite toy: used, torn and loved.

And there, beside the word 'inchoate' lay of bit of Lebanon.

Seven pine needles. Crisp and sage lay within.

And the floods crashed through.

Opening up endless views, colours and smells.

Outside the main house by the playground,

Boys mingling, talking in the freezing air of sixty three.

Kennedy was our false idol then under those very trees.

Little did we know what the future held.

Fifteen years. Another three of those or so

And the seeds of our talk would be full grown.

Grown to much less than there was then.

Much less. Like all those growing young.

All innocent gone. All plans forgot. All fears grown.

Ah! All our little dreams screaming out:

That was no country for little boys.

And now?

This is *"no country for old men"*.

Sailing to England I

Where *"they're all mad there"*.

Thank God.

Palestinian coin, unknown photographer.

COH

To my distant Cyrillic family who speak no Russian yet.

Little buds out turned so that the snow would not recognise them.

A few sharp green heads getting ready to loll in a fine breeze.

The grass is green. Especially on the other side of our lives.

There stands a cottage with white buds, sharp green heads and

That greenest of green green grass that tells of rotation.

Memories rotate and smile with a heart laden with sorrow.

That grass looks so green in the moving windscreen saying

Over and over again: "*One day it will be very green and then trust will*

sprout with life."

Laid back saying nothing anymore. Looking through the windscreen
there is a pretence that

It is the window of a future life through green sliding curtains and green
leather bound

Volumes. All is green and a little some blue with a few reds.

Makes the colour of a short story where characters do not

Really live or feel or get hurt or trust their love to anyone but

That foolish author who thinks all is not impossible if he really

Wants it. All, that is, except that it is not all green and it is

Not all trust. Alone in a darkened room bursting for hurt, shame and
loneliness.

Something dies inside. The windscreen shatters and the window

On that dream goes dark. Just able to see the garden with

Its sloping edges going nowhere in the dark. Standing by

The edge was that vision. He used to call it epiphany and make

Them laugh at his quirky smirking fancy seeing things no one

Wanted to see. Standing by the edge was him. Younger, stronger, in

control.

Saying over and over again, "*Never again*". How many men had

Said that before him and laughed at themselves afterwards

In Florence, Venice, Beirut or Paris? Paris. How he hates that

Name. He used to call it epiphany and make them laugh at his

Quirky smirking fancy seeing things no one wanted to see.

All the horrors seen and the misfortunes dodged aimlessly

Fruitlessly because being seen is being there and being

There is seeing again that which was already seen. But one vision was

pure. And he

Found it not in a green grassy knoll where Oswald was not or in a

green "*many*

Splendoured" field where no one was. He found it in a crowded room

where

All was as green and as blue as red ever can be. And it no

Longer mattered what Florence brought. What Paris wrought.

What Beirut thought. Until tonight. Standing by a darkened window

looking out and talking to himself. Blubbering words like that time a

million years

Ago. Crying with an aloneness that no Lucifer could but

Pity. No destroyer of lives but feel saddened by.

It was cold that night. It was freezing cold. It was lonely. It was

endlessly lonely.

It was icy hearts and fearsome darkness without end.

And the garden remained shrouded in the dark until the morning

When he said "*Good morning*" as if Kennedy had not been killed and

Oswald had

Actually done it. Which he hadn't. But he will carry that little silly

Vision to his grave. Because his life is suddenly

Meaningless, good morninged and sad. The morning was not good

because it was dark.

Kennedy's book lay in a spongy drawer afraid to show

His face for fear fumigating fulminating froth forth that day in Dallas.

In the afternoon he visited the garden and smiled.

Because it was still dark. Very dark. And will always be

The same. For something died last night. And, like Kennedy,

Once dead; it takes a courageous human being

To bring it back to life in a green and blue

And very red garden.

Goodbye dream world. Hello epiphany once again.

Kennedy – and I – are gone now. Forever.

And so, lifelong ambition's end,
Not world changing, mind shaking,
Writing for eternity why and how to be.
Just content. Happy to be me.

FHM
22.06.04

'Happy to Be Me', drawn and written by the poet.

Lebanese Roulette

[Started July 1982

Finished June 2014]

A heavy load crushes my vertical body,

saddening by the fire and sad.

This is act three hundred and six

of that tragi-comedy we call peace.

Heat intolerable bubbles behind. Before,

a cold like the dark side of the moon.

A lethargy. So dull thudding in

my weary eyes calcified.

I turn over and think

If Everest ever had to turn over, it

would feel like this

Heavy

Dull

Rumbling and

    dis

satisfied.

Now the dark side of the moon is

boiling.

The sun has set on my back.

This is hard. A hard life. I undress with the minimum of

effort. A kind of mental atrophy. Wasting. Wasting. Wasting.

I am warm. My bowels relax.

A pain is somewhere but no longer

in me.

I feel my limpness painfully.

"*I have found a new way to masturbate,*" he said

smiling through the telephone piece

after telling me that he had AIDS

which in ten years, they say now in 1982,

as I lay by the fire, would hit someone you love.

Not me, I thought.

Not with her and me loving so.

Even that, an effort. Jerk. Jerk.

Jerking off.

It's a sin. What do Catholics call it?

"*I'm a catlick. I'm a catlick.*" I can still hear her voice.

So Irish. I loved it.

And I can still see my vision of her being a catlick

And I licking her pussy.

But that was before he told me that he had AIDS.

I remember my first time:

lying on my stomach

rubbing myself on the sheets

and wondering what would happen

next.

I mumbled something through it all

though it

could not have been obscene.

May be it was "*mummy*".

Since she was dead: it was:

ob-scene.

I remember thinking that this was

too much work for too little

reward:

a spurt and a shimper.

A panicking. The sheets.

Till I remembered: normally you

would have a woman there. The

sheets would be safe.

Oh my soul – my little defenceless soul

What broke you in two

And took one half away?

What fractured the remaining half and let it stay?

Oh my little soul

Where will I ever find that other half to mend my life

And make me whole once again?

I cry bitter tears for you my soul and

for her who carries that other half and waits for the accident

that will one day make us one.

Come near my other half soul. Come to me. Wherever you are.

There is no woman there.

That too was before he died of drink

and then he got AIDS and my sister drank

and our father went senile and died.

But then he was always senile the fascist bastard,

the jackbooted emotionally stunted beast.

So, I set out looking for

wom-man.

Oh how I love that play on words

the womb and the man and the woman all in one.

Trying with words to find that other half of me and failing so

desperately.

I was thirteen.

I found one, I thought. She was

twenty eight

She made me do things then,

as a reward;

she buggered me with her finger and jerked me off

and ordered me to come –

without shutting my eyes

nipple mouthed mouthing "*mummy*"

whimpering.

She said my eyes sparkled as I came

and stroked her little baby with his half soul.

Oh my fractured and my broken soul

cry with me if you can.

And she gave me a grade 'A' for my English essay.

And then passed me on to the music teacher

Who... Oh my little soul, give me peace, I pray you.

They call it child abuse now

and tell me that I should have never enjoyed any of it.

It has not changed; as I

whimpered and lay arched – my

prick hanged convicted for obscenity

through endless years of whimpering.

"*You have such soft hands...*

Your brain must be badly blistered, my love."

She smiled and held me tight

Forty-six to her twenty years

in a clean Brighton room at the top

with her smile nibbling at my eyes.

It was, I think, a last birthday party before he was to die

of AIDS.

Mother. Brother. Father. And now him.

Of AIDS.

He laughed at the life to come after he went.

Called father a shit for leaving us so little money.

And when the time came for him to die,

I held his left hand, covered in leaking sores

And watched his blinding eyes

And tried to tell him how I loved him

And promised to do what he asked

To die with dignity and to keep

that bitch away from his space.

Yet, when he died, she ran in screaming

And I held her tight and lied to her about how I loved her

And how I would care for her

From now onwards

The vicious callous nasty bitch.

But, my soul, I have not the courage

To hurt even those I hate so.

My little soul, all I ask for is someone to love me as I am

And I her as she is

For she would be your other half

My little sad broken soul.

And then to hold her in my arms as I wait

so when she assents, I fill her with my love and

vow endless words – I know not what they will be

because they will be hers and not mine

if she exists – and my half soul says she does.

And he still called father a shit for leaving us with so little money

less life and least character.

And I wondered backwards and forwards

through life's narrow and wide lanes.

"Your wife has a screw loose

my dear brother. Tell the children that

they have not lost a mum

They have found a new house

in leafy Wiltshire.

There their mother enjoys the new screw

that makes her loose one firm

right up her sad lamented and lost vagina.

You still love her

my sad lamented and lost brother

and she couldn't do more than wish you dead.

Voilà.

You've really got problems loving her so.

Than God I've only got AIDS.

I know where I am going

and, it's not Dubai where the buggers threw me out

because I have AIDS

little do they know that it is their brains that are diseased

from history's solicitations.

Blind, I can see further than you

or her or that Biblical bastard that stole her from you."

I cried and he looked embarrassed

told me that I would one day kill myself

and see my old loves

unless I could find that other half of my poor poor stolen soul.

That was before she came to me and asked to make love one more

time

Asked if she could have my mouth

And I, desperate for warmth, said yes.

And as she lay there satisfied she looked at me and

Asked, "*Oh my darling, did you swallow every drop of my love*?"

I nodded and she laughed and

Said

"*That was him inside me. Oh how I loved fucking two men in one day.*

Now, hit me. Hit me. Hit me."

And I got up, looking foolish,

Went to the bathroom and was sick

Dressed quickly

Drove her home to him

Shook her hand goodbye

And never saw her again.

Hitting is not my style

Neither is it yours my poor abused half soul.

My brother, well he knew where he was going

and he will see her there for sure.

Father was a cardboard. I craved for his approval

and love

and got his dispassion and his creamed hair sticking statically aloft.

Mother we didn't know. Brother laughed his life through the bottle and

died.

Sister replaced mother and we loved her with an intense

Hatred. Hatred. Hatred.

She took me to the top floor and told me to look out of the window

Across the road, through the window, lay a man

His hand moving so fast I could not understand

And she breathed heavily and told me that we men were disgusting

And I did not understand what I had done

As the man arched himself and did a wee wee I thought.

Brother is now dying of AIDS.

And I wondered what I will die of

thinking that this will be read and probably the reader will then

know

poor man, of a broken heart and a fractured soul

methinks and because

she gave him her loose screw.

And I wonder still if, when I die, my soul's little mate

Will hold my little hand and tell me that she loved me

And will love me still after I am dead.

Oh my soul, I doubt it

he is right, I fear, I will, one day, kill myself

for death holds no terrors for half souls

as long as the other half still lives somewhere

In China, Russia or Peru.

What are the chances of two half souls meeting, my dear friend?

And then when I die

They will converse by my corporeal remains

with my reader and probably the reader will

know

poor man, of a broken heart he died

because she gave him her loose screw.

Oh, he was no angel

a shit really

who joked a lot

wouldn't hurt a fly

and meant no harm

learning her love for a hundred years

and listening to her strong hug and protection.

His innocence killed him.

He meant well – the fool.

And he died loving her

the fool.

But then – his poetry ain't bad really.

If you like that sort of thing

depressing and gory and dirty

made her mother cringe that she did not marry

that nice man next door

instead of a child

and then a

bastard she liked so.

Whimpering years.

Through endless years of whimpering.

Everest was snowcapped. I

turned and the snow burned and

ran down molten digits. My

watch face burnt. Eight-thirty.

Like some atomised Hiroshima.

Like that time at the De Vere Hotel

When she watched the snow stream down his shaft

And told him not to move so that she can look at it carefully

"*God,*" she said, "*You have a beautiful prick*

and it glistens so my love, it glistens so

after you've come."

And he hid his face in embarrassment

And she laughed at his embarrassment given how he talked – the

naunny boy.

That clock like some atomised Hiroshima.

and the fall-out invisible life.

I threw my watch in the fire because:

It was there

and I was coming.

Sylvialike I could now call my father a "*bastard*"

with his jack booted brains and murderous love.

At eight-thirty September twenty-eighth mid nineties

Smiling at me and saying she loved me

little knowing what I had seen.

"*I have betrayed you my love*

I have".

And I, calm in three month shock

asked "*with whom*?"

ever so grammatically correct

and the Biblical name flew out

soiled and soiling.

And from then onwards

the knife once in

they twisted it endlessly

endlessly

endlessly.

Endlessly – till there was no more blood

and plenty of excuses

for my guilt. And execution.

"*Blind. Blind. Blind*".

But never mind. You have recovered now.

She has given you your sight back.

And I washed my new eyes over and over again

As he mumbled embarrassed love.

Like Maria – with her Brighton love

so short. So quick. So powerful.

Running away to Alison

to be the Biblical bastard

I

and take her away from

her nest.

"You are still wonderful

but you love her and I

live in no little one's shadow".

What a neat circle.

Rebecca reversed.

I lay like Milton's fallen

angel predestined knowing wrong

helpless to stand once fallen.

I well remember how, as a child of

twenty-four, I shouted to

Faustus to ask forgiveness

even as the firmament turned red

    with

    the

    drip blood drip

    of

    Christ

    Jesu

and felt stupid when they all looked

at me.

And that night I made Mary

come while we talked

murder

In Lewes in a seedy London hotel.

She was a gift she said.

"*From your brother*".

And I was barely out of my teens.

"*Lie back sweetheart and let me pleasure you*

you brother would kill me if I did not blow your brain

with this – it's good, isn't it my love?"

Those were the sixties when we thought

we knew it all and felt it all

and wanted to drink life to the lees

and leaving not a drop to chance.

Whatever happened to equal opportunities

and respect for women?

choice?

She said to me, "*Ah! Men are men and women are women and*

let's cut the crap. Fuck me again like a man".

And I was confused

and have been since then

especially after Germaine Greer sexed me

so long in the mid seventies

and explained why women were equal

and I loved her so, that I agreed and never let go

of a woman's right to be herself and no one else.

But every time they tell that I am wrong

I am filled with doubt and hate women for

doing this to us. Or did we do it?

I give up and hide.

In Germaine Greer's little farm in Essex where she

taught me the art of pleasuring my loves

and rewarded me in ways unmentionable.

After Lewes in London

We had steak, salad and spring onions

and I cringe to think what we did with our food.

But she drew the line at food in Lewes

and I never asked because of respect.

"*I'm a catlick.*" And I never asked.

She explained the Trinity and I never asked.

That was a long time ago

Long before I gave up planning what to do

when I grow up

and

retire.

One day I shall have four fires:

One at each wall and I in the

middle.

That would save on turning.

And I fell asleep.

And had the oddest dream.

of three poems.

to Louise:

marry me and let us live on the prairie have a daughter and perhaps

call her mary and every night i'll spurt spunk right up your cunt and

we'll be happy middleclassed you surely must punt

to jennie:

marry me and let us live on the prairie have a daughter and perhaps

call her mary and every night i'll squirt right up you arse and we'll be

happy middleclassed your greenness grass

and to my little wife the bitch to be:

marry me and let us live on the prairie have a daughter and perhaps

call her mary and every night i'll

and I woke up screaming and crying. Embarrassed.

Not my wife.

The rhyme. The rhyme. So bloody awful.

That time in New York

on the ground looking up at the South Tower

with my second wife sulking

calling me names and insisting on me taking her back to the hotel

"*I want to watch you fuck a prostitute tonight.*"

And when I refused, she screamed at me

And said she wished the Twin Towers would fall on me

and I thought how neat that would be because she stood right beside

me.

And we went back to the hotel and she invited the pretty barmaid

downstairs.

I went for a walk burning with excitement tinged with shame.

And still said no.

When I came back, they were in bed together, in deep drunken sleep.

And I slept in the bar downstairs and took a long early morning walk

With her telephone call of over one year later

On the eleventh of September 2001 crying

"*You were my soul mate, come back to me my darling love.*"

Come back and forgive me all my ills. It was the drink love. Not me."

I cried as I said no and put the phone down.

And a week later I collapsed in lovely Paris

and suffered something not tangible and almost fulfilled my brother's

prophecy

till the medicos took me off to a nice quiet place to recover

and then on to Malta.

I thought of Helen. Water bubbled

by her face.

"I don't mind an affair though let's

cut the romantic crap".

"It's my idea of your dick that I dig. What do you think?"

Before a new disease came that they said

burnt your brains slowly and

had Whitehouse saying

"I told you so".

And she told me that she found it hard

to fuck

instead of making love

and say words like 'cunt'

instead of just coming

after a quiet walk in the woods.

Little knowing what I did see.

Four letter words must never be said.

But they can be done

in front of open fires

in the front room

on the family's hearth…

They killed cheerfully

and condemned me for saying

'Fuck'.

That was before the authorities in Dubai hurt me

and threw my brother out because he had AIDS

and sent him to me to die by my side.

I taught for years in some crappy Ipswich school

where more lying to children

cheating of parents

and destroying of lives took place than

did in that old old Russia.

I have nightmares about it now.

Somewhere. We had been reading poems.

Somehow. Putney bridge did not

seem like the ideal place to cheat

on my wife duffeled up with a

melody in her very walk.

But she's grown a bitch of late

what with brother's AIDS and alcohol and hate

is frightened to enjoy her life

because of all that terrible strife

since she became a Christian if you please and

what's more – a Samaritan

she has hated all the fun of being man or woman.

Till the Biblical bastard walked by

destroyed all

and she – Christian if you please – forgave him

the cry for help

and let him fuck to his heart's content

and lied till the lies became others' truths.

That once so kind woman whose

happiness is like a sunflower.

She is a simile and I that

awful conceit that confuses her

and me

so.

I stood by my pupil looking at her tearful face

And asked her what the matter was

"Oh sir. Sir. I love you so much".

And I called the pastoral care woman and told her

And she took Michelle away.

I asked for her to be moved from my literature class.

And ten years later I collapsed in Birmingham

as my wife told me she was no more

and all was at an end.

And there in the little hospital was the little one grown

"Sir. Sir. You remember me?"

Of course I remember you my little one.

And we made love on the hospital bed and her hand on my mouth

To stop the moans

For fear of being caught.

And six months later on Avebury Hill she slapped me hard

Made love for the last time on the grass

And went off to Australia.

"Sir. Sir. You bastard. I love you so, I love you so. Bastard."

Adultery must be grand.

In a cottage.

With a fire.

In Ireland. Its west coast. The crash of waves.

Smell of horse.

Sweat.

Bloody provoking passion-filled.

After the kill.

Like that Ireland begging before begged

and that night in Edington

three to four doors

down I made love to

"*klikkaklakkaklaskaklopatzklatschabattacreppycrottygraddaahsemmihs*

ammihonithaappluddyyappladdypkonpkot"

which of course explains it all thoroughly

back in 1922

in Paris capital city of Ireland.

I lay on my back again.

And thought I would jump up, run in, grab the

Work

"*Irish oldpan retold early in*" firefront

penis again waiting

Execution

Riverrun.

When my brother looked at me and

Challenged me to sleep with both sisters within a week

And he would give me one thousand pounds and all expenses paid.

Oh, the arrogance of youth.

The cruelty of youth.

I worked so hard

It was a dizzying time aged barely seventeen or eighteen

So dizzying that I did not even enjoy sleeping with each

And the mother caught me with the second

Got angry

And took me to her bed.

The stupidity of youth

Well before – well before

I became a decent man.

And oh my soul, I try so hard to be good.

So hard.

Oh Lord, help me find the other half soul. And I would be safe.

Warm.

Happy.

Fulfilled.

And I had thought that I had won the bet

and was happy with the thousand pounds

little knowing that the real bet was the three women

making my penis sore and my brain befuddled with the porridge of

stupidity.

I lay on my back again.

And thought I would jump up, run in, grab the

work

"*Irish oldpan retold in*" firefront

penis again waiting

Execution

riverrun.

I remembered it though I lack

a memory

because my brother's AIDS virus is so small

that it goes into my brother's brain

after the fascist bastards threw him out of little Dubai

that fun fair on the sea

filled with cruelty and such such ineffable beauty.

But his life with a knot on my finger

I drummed it out

"*riverrun, past Eve and Adam's, from swerve of shore and bend of bay,*

brings us by a commodious vicus of recirculation back to Howth Castle

and Environs."

The most beautiful lines in English

Irish

Swiss

Zurichois

literature.

Where Einstein and I spent many happy hours

Before I explained Relativity and died of Cancer.

There is a compromise for you, reader.

You damned hypocrite.

Let's be havin' it again mate:

"*riverrun, past Eve and Adam's, from swerve of shore and bend of bay,*

brings us by a commodious vicus of recirculation back to Howth Castle

and Environs."

The most beautiful lines in English

Irish

Swiss

Zurichois

literature.

Where Einstein and I spent many happy hours

Before I explained Relativity and died of Cancer.

There is a compromise for you, reader.

You damned hypocrite.

Let's be havin' it again mate:

"*riverrun, past Eve and Adam's, from swerve of shore and bend of bay,*

brings us by a commodious vicus of recirculation back to Howth Castle

and Environs."

The most beautiful lines in English

Irish

Swiss

Zurichois

literature.

Where Einstein and I spent many happy hours

Before I explained Relativity and died of Cancer.

There is a compromise for you, reader.

You damned hypocrite.

Let's be havin' it again mate:

"riverrun, past Eve and Adam's, from swerve of shore and bend of bay,

brings us by a commodious vicus of recirculation back to Howth Castle

and Environs."

The most beautiful lines in English

Irish

Swiss

Zurichois

literature.

Where Einstein and I spent many happy hours

Before I explained Relativity and died of Cancer.

There is a compromise for you, reader.

You damned hypocrite.

Let's be havin' it again mate:

"riverrun, past Eve and Adam's, from swerve of shore and bend of bay,

brings us by a commodious vicus of recirculation back to Howth Castle

and Environs."

The most beautiful lines in English

Irish

Swiss

Zurichois

literature.

Where Einstein and I spent many happy hours

Before I explained Relativity and died of Cancer.

There is a compromise for you, reader.

You damned hypocrite.

Let's be havin' it again mate:

No more.

Why did you repeat it so many times then my poet?

Well, you see it was 1995 or 2001 and I had little to say

and in all these cases I got together with Joyce, Einstein,

Dickens or Shakespeare and they said it for me.

So, how many nervous break downs did you have?

I never had a nervous break down.

I was suffering from Severe Post Traumatic Stress Disorder.

SPTSD. Oh how I love the little abbreviations – the little letters.

No more.

As my poor ductile soon pendulous

pendant

shimpered

"*darling*".

Or was it again

"*Mummy*"?

"Why on earth are all your short stories with boys?

Don't women exist in your world?"

What prophetic words my dear!

So I went home and using my new computer

searched and sliced every penis

replaced all

hes with shes

all boys with girls

all men with women

all Pauls with Maggies

and Davids with Julies

and when you go to Florence's Accademia di Belle Arti

(Oooh! That lovely language – so… contrapposto)

you will now see Micheangelo's

'Julie' and her catapult which destroyed Goliath

and I became the champion of

EEEEEEEEEEEEEEEEEEEEE

OOOOOOOOOOOOOOOOOO

Hurrah!!

Always do the exact opposite of what women say

in running affairs of state said a great vizier once.

Precursor of Machiavelli with optimism and some fun.

He may have been wrong. Always do what

they say and hide the rest.

But then where's Hilary Clinton in all this?

She will never be President the poor cove.

So divorce Bill and make a new life for yourself.

You will not be in the Casa Blanca.

and again mate if you please:

"*riverrun, past Eve and Adam's, from swerve of shore and bend of bay,*

brings us by a commodious vicus of recirculation back to Howth Castle

and Environs."

The most beautiful lines in English

Irish

Swiss

Zurichois

literature.

Where Einstein and I spent many happy hours

Before I explained Relativity and died of Cancer.

There is a compromise for you, reader.

You damned hypocrite.

Let's be havin' it again mate:

"riverrun, past Eve and Adam's, from swerve of shore and bend of bay,

brings us by a commodious vicus of recirculation back to Howth Castle

and Environs."

The most beautiful lines in English

Irish

Swiss

Zurichois

literature.

Where Einstein and I spent many happy hours

Before I explained Relativity and died of Cancer.

There is a compromise for you, reader.

You damned hypocrite.

Let's be havin' it again mate:

That's enough for now.

Let us return to our little sheepsies:

Some would have it that poor Maggie

needed a vizier like this one and perhaps

she wouldn't have become a lady so soon.

Which she was before anyhow.

When she invited me to tea to discuss my manuscript

of her life

so ineffably patronising, so kind and so huskily gentle

and that silk handkerchief excited my imagination

that I almost could see sex with her

smell it

as I said "*of course, Baroness. Yes Baroness.*

I'm so pleased you like it…"

"*But I don't. It's awful. Let Whittingdale help you my boy.*

I so hate those women's libbers with their strident tones

and why don't you vote for me?"

So they did and proved that a dickhead

is not always the best

whatever men think.

Awakened and slightly shamed

I said:

"*Oh my male organ of musicality*

Prime Minister

Vizier

Thou (for we are on familiar name terms)

needst some psycho-analytic analysis."

Oh my gentle gentle soul

Be still

Stay calm

Your other half roams the earth and will soon be found.

Talk not to that pusillanimous penis

penitentially silent except for saying

"You turn if you want to

this baby's not for turning".

Oh I love those little clever puns

they hide so little in so much

and tell you

years later

that what happened had already started

when you wrote those little words then

and read them so long later on.

"Life's but a dream" whence

words spoken today

some in jest others in earnest

come rolling back after the event

showing what you wouldn't see

when you first gave birth to them

and thought you were clever. Hypocrite.

And blind.

And again mate if you don't mind:

"*riverrun, past Eve and Adam's, from swerve of shore and bend of bay,*

brings us by a commodious vicus of recirculation back to Howth Castle

and Environs."

The most beautiful lines in English

Irish

Swiss

Zurichois

literature.

Where Einstein and I spent many happy hours

Before I explained Relativity and died of Cancer.

There is a compromise for you, reader.

You damned hypocrite.

Let's be havin' it again mate:

"*riverrun, past Eve and Adam's, from swerve of shore and bend of bay,*

brings us by a commodious vicus of recirculation back to Howth Castle

and Environs."

The most beautiful lines in English

Irish

Swiss

Zurichois

literature.

Where Einstein and I spent many happy hours

Before I explained Relativity and died of Cancer.

There is a compromise for you, reader.

You damned hypocrite.

Let's be havin' it again mate:

Enough.

"*riverrun, past Eve and Adam's, from swerve of shore and bend of bay,*

brings us by a commodious vicus of recirculation back to Howth Castle

and Environs."

The most beautiful lines in English

Irish

Swiss

Zurichois

literature.

Where Einstein and I spent many happy hours

Before I explained Relativity and died of Cancer.

There is a compromise for you, reader.

You damned hypocrite.

Let's be havin' it again mate:

Enough. I say enough.

"riverrun, past Eve and Adam's, from swerve of shore and bend of bay,

brings us by a commodious vicus of recirculation back to Howth Castle

and Environs."

The most beautiful lines in English

Irish

Swiss

Zurichois

literature.

Where Einstein and I spent many happy hours

Before I explained Relativity and died of Cancer.

There is a compromise for you, reader.

You damned hypocrite.

Let's be havin' it again mate:

"riverrun, past Eve and Adam's, from swerve of shore and bend of bay,

brings us by a commodious vicus of recirculation back to Howth Castle

and Environs."

The most beautiful lines in English

Irish

Swiss

Zurichois

literature.

Where Einstein and I spent many happy hours

Before I explained Relativity and died of Cancer.

There is a compromise for you, reader.

You damned hypocrite.

Let's be havin' it again mate:

ENOUGH! This is dangerous for you know not

what dark secrets those prophetic words hide

to be seen

in years to come.

That is how life's joined and punctuated

the coma here full stop there

of life

are but words

that hit you so hard when you lose your sight

and mind

and

the one you so loved

all those years.

You poor creat-toor as we Frenchies say.

ENOUGH.

If you come again mate I'll go home and write no more secrets.

Oh! Oh! My simple soul. Fear not, my love.

Your other half still roams and will soon be there

And you will be whole and all will be whole.

As my friend said, two halves. "*Reason not the need*".

"*I am more sinned against than sinning*".

For no harm have I done.

No hurt have I caused.

No hatred have I carried.

Give me the rest of my soul now.

Take my hurts away.

This baby's not for turning.

"*What a pellicle*," methought poetically.

and turned towards the fire.

I heard him speak over the music and the shouting.

His nurse held him gently and he said,

"*I have a life to live.*

I know that I am going to die.

But I have a life to live.

A fucking good life."

I felt tired and embarrassed. Tired of

AIDS carried by others and not by me.

Almost envious of their love and liberty.

Embarrassed for being clean and envious

of not knowing when and how to die.

And I cried in the nurse's arms

As she stroked my hair and told me to cry my heart out

And not to feel shame

As I sobbed and sobbed and Mohammad stood beside me praying

And at the funeral I refused to enter the mosque

With Mohammad standing by me and telling all to go

and leave me alone

smoking cigarette after cigarette till feeling sick

and the body they prayed for was not his

but some poor woman

whose son accosted me all shy and mortified

and asked if we could swap coffins

for there had been a clerical error at the morgue.

I hugged him and we swapped

His mum for my brother

And I cried by the gaping graveside amidst an occasional laugh at the

mistake

"Poor man. His brother's death has unhinged him.

He died in his arms you know."

In Beirut when the fighting dies

down when people come out

and

    play. When.

One game is old by a new

not

    very

       original

name.

Lebanese Roulette.

In Russia we had four chances in five to live.

In Beirut you have but one chance

in five to die. Now –

I need the Russo-Lebanese version.

If I went to Battersea park.

If I spun the chamber.

If I cocked the hammer.

If I pulled the trigger (somebody

told me once that it is the

trigger that pulls the finger – but then

that was bad English as you trow).

I speak bad German at times.

Like that psychiatrist I met in Malta

who spoke nothing but German

and told me about her dead husband

and we went for a walk on the cliff

and made love in a cave

away from my daughter's protective eyes.

That night I skulked down the corridor like a thief

and groped for her bedroom

where we held on tight as she spoke in German

and I could not understand but knew that she was urging me

and I, being a good soldier, complied

and felt so tired.

I was very ill then

recovering in Malta

and sleeping with my German friend.

Oh my soul, I digress again.

I diverge – that di is like you split in two

and your other half wondering the earth

in search of you as you are of her.

Diverging is a way out.

"*In the room the women come and go*

Talking of Michelangelo"

"*O O O O that Shakespeherian Rag*" –

we recited such nonsense in cafés

in the sixties

and talked politics

and planned our lives and the world's future.

One day the plan was ready and

we stood prepared to carry it out.

But life had slipped out for a while.

I have diverged, my soul. I have.

If I went to Hyde Park

If I spun the chamber

If I cocked the hammer

If I pulled the trigger

If

If

What if I felt a little scratch on

my little temple?

What if I died?

What next?

Blood spurts a long arch that

Circularises.

The way it did so long ago when I walked through the bomb

explosion.

Legs then give way and I fold

fold

crumbling

the dark side of the moon

crumbles

slowly

blackly

bloodily.

When found.

No matter.

Children orphaned.

Will my daughter finger herself

and whimper 'daddy'?

If?

Then that sullied bitch should be home and dry

and can have all heart's desire

fire, hearth and the new loose screw.

If?

But what if I just hear a little

click and my temple intact?

What if?

The triumph of having courted

death and won.

The adrenaline flowing coursing

coursing coursing through my

new life.

Like a virus uncaught.

The excitement of the risk and the

gamble.

The love of the game and

the game of the love

causes this.

The ennui destroyed with one click.

One in five.

What is after the loss?

I couldn't – as I faced my fire

again. Knowing that brother's AIDS abets my life in a conspiracy of knowing unknown death.

Soon it will need new logs.

I am in truth cowardly.

I will play Russian Roulette

with

    an

        empty

            gun – I like it better than

            revolver.

I remembered that time when my brother's friend shot himself

through the head with an empty gun

in 1961.

Or thereabouts in midplans.

In Beirut. Or Dublin.

Perhaps Russian Roulette is silly,

Stay away from guns my boy.

You might die. Or even worse get hurt. In a mess.

We picked a man up once. He kept worrying about the

blood and the mess it made on the Opel upholstery.

He died and we couldn't get the fucking blood off.

When I was six I sat on the garage roof and watched

the Easter uprising.

In Beirut to the West of Ireland.

One heroic fool charged and died.

We clapped

God forgive us for callous infants,

We clapped

The neighbours washed their balcony and pink water gurgled out.

I asked my mum

and she said that he was dead.

Now what's that exactly?

Gone.

How?

Into shit.

and I told dad that she said a bad word.

He laughed.

Really. I thought.

I liked it when he laughed because then he didn't beat the shit out of

us.

They say some men come when

they're hanged.

I mean. Bitter taste.

Imagine. Smoke filled.

A naked man about to be hanged.

For not planning his life with proper words.

He was illiterate you see.

His wife holds on to his legs. Trying to keep life in.

The trap goes.

His prick spurts its last as his neck clicks.

She looks up

Shocked

Helpless

       Frightened.

Lost.

His last sign of life as

she hangs on

A Lebanese soldier once hung kindly on to an executed one's legs

after they had kicked for fifteen minutes… I saw it in 1916. On the

television. I wasn't even born then. And we didn't have a television in

1916. Father said it was bad for us. And we couldn't afford it anyhow

on account of them bloody Ottomans…

She grabs his penis and catches

his sperm

to rough

up her

    may be a son or daughter one day

like him.

The soldiers laugh as she pushes her moist fingers in.

The Ottoman flag flying majestically

for that sick man of Europe.

And her son?

He will probably die of AIDS in London or Paris

and everyone will notch him up for a new statistic.

All her love and plans his plan and loves

in a virus so small – minuscule. What a lovely word.

"Am I standing up straight, nuncle?"

said the little Jewish boy to

his uniformed Nazi who smiled

and patted him on the large head

and then shot him through it – once.

And they say that Himmler flinched with disgust as a bit of brain

soiled his immaculate ugly uniform.

And forty years later,

yet unborn

soiled her knickers

as the bullets shredded her

tiny

tiny

minuscule

body

so often kidded and kissed and cuddled and caressed.

One Israeli bullet

Made in the USA

"*Our father who art in Heaven*"

please say the prayer with me.

All is ember and ash now.

The fire is almost out.

My body is all the dark side

of the moon

    and I cannot

be bothered

to throw

little logs.

To explain how Europe grew

and how I was born in the city of Beirut in County Cork with two late

brothers, one half late sister and two late parents.

So I fall asleep and dream of

going to bed and falling asleep

and of dreaming

of going to bed and

of.

The mirror effect enlarges

and expands my lack of

movement.

I live in the mirror.

People can not tell the difference.

When the fire is out and my dear wife sweeps the ash

for we haven't parted yet

that is in the future of those sad rambling words

and in her rotten

mother's brain

sweeps the ash

that contains my burnt

babies

unborn

and my dreams

and our plans

and their lost lives

unborn.

And little Emma

asking to be born

in the corner of the new kitchen.

When all that and a little more happens.

I still have my mirrors.

My dreams.

My verses that took a quarter of a century to write.

One more time then mate – it is so beautiful:

"riverrun, past Eve and Adam's, from swerve of shore and bend of bay,

brings us by a commodious vicus of recirculation back to Howth Castle

and Environs."

The most beautiful lines in English

Irish

Swiss

Zurichois

literature.

Where Einstein and I spent many happy hours

Before I explained Relativity and died of Cancer.

There is a compromise for you, reader.

You damned hypocrite.

I did warn you

"*riverrun, past Eve and Adam's, from swerve of shore and bend of bay, brings us by a commodious vicus of recirculation back to Howth Castle and Environs.*"

The most beautiful lines in English

Irish

Swiss

Zurichois

literature.

Where Einstein and I spent many happy hours

Before I explained Relativity and died of Cancer.

There is a compromise for you, reader.

You damned hypocrite.

Let's be havin' it again mate:

"*riverrun, past Eve and Adam's, from swerve of shore and bend of bay, brings us by a commodious vicus of recirculation back to Howth Castle and Environs.*"

The most beautiful lines in English

Irish

Swiss

Zurichois

literature.

Where Einstein and I spent many happy hours

Before I explained Relativity and died of Cancer.

There is a compromise for you, reader.

You damned hypocrite.

Let's be havin' it again mate:

Mate?

Oh come on mate. Be a sport.

Come on.

Hey?

"And your brother died of AIDS? Do you know what that means?"

"What will people say, my friend?"

"*Mon frère, mon semblable, mon hypocrite*".

For now, my soul, the end draws near and we are at home

And I can tell you the good news.

I left Beirut so long ago I no longer remember when

I left to search for the other half of my fractured half soul.

I searched near and I searched far

I searched inside my life and I tried outside

And I never found your other half, my sad forlorn soul.

And then, irony of irony, in Beirut,

I asked if we were falling in love

and then you fluttered

and I walked all night

and refused to see

that now you were whole

my little, my tired, my fractured, my ever loyal

soul.

Whole.

Whole.

Whole.

My soul.

Whole at last.

Whole at last.

Where?

Who?

I can not see

for the half found

joined that half that had died.

Whole at last.

Whole at last.

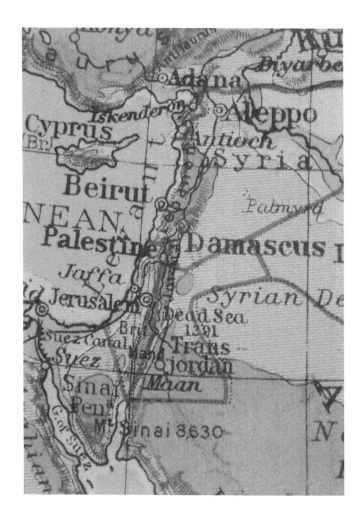

'Map of Palestine', *Philips' Elementary Atlas of Comparative Geography*, George

Philip and Son, Ltd., London, 1945.

A Return: The Siege of Beirut was first published by Martin Brian and O'Keeffe, ISBN: 0 85616 291 4, London, 1983. This edition is currently out of print.

Extracts from *A Return: The Siege of Beirut* were also published by Yorick Books: Lomax, Marion (Editor), *Time Present and Time Past*, 1985, ISBN 0 9477 103 5.

A Return: The Siege of Beirut

Book 1: The Dying

1

I wish to go out and love some woman.

I wish to go out and make a child.

I wish to go out and spend my money.

I wish to go out and be a madman.

I wish to go out and smoke for fullness.

All this I wish, and more, because it is

The eternal 'I' that will live on beyond

All this. And when they die and their

bodies are motionless and hard and the

Bulldozers shuffle them, Jewlike, to their grave;

I wish that I, too, could be there to feel

their pain and taste the bloodied dust.

All this I wish and more: so much more.

2

To the late Marwan Sidani

When we were little we went out

to hunt. We shot birds that were

smaller still and stared back with

white empty eyes, heads lolling and

bodies warmly tender.

We ate oranges and sucked melons

all red and bloodied.

Our tummies rumbled and our heads

tumbled. No war for us. A sport:

shooting birds.

The birds are gone. The guns rust.

We are grown men now, feeling and seeming.

War is a rumble and some smoke;

a ball of fire that soon goes out.

Sounds, noises, and white eyes, empty

heads lolling and bodies warmly tender.

War is a siege; a concrete tumbling

and heads all red and bloodied.

Kill us, my friend, and turn us back.

Your rumbles tumbles and bloodied

balls of fire will turn against you

My friend.

For the very breast whose milk you have soured

With fear, hatred, bitterness, and death,

Will suckle the babe whose life be dowered –

His health, wealth, and your very death.

3

I thought I dreamt of home last night.

Olive orchards, citrus groves, sweet smelling and ageless.

I thought too that my people were there.

Young and old with serene and quiet look.

They had won the battle, I thought.

They are home – home at last.

I helped rebuild a city.

We called it Jerusalem.

All this I dreamt and a little more.

I met an elder with a baby in his arms.

Is this home?

And he replied. No, my friend,

this is the afterlife. We all died

in war.

This *is* our Jerusalem.

And I dreamt of home and of

cheating death last of all.

4

Once I asked my mother about Jerusalem.

She laughed and said shalom aley-kem.

I laughed too. I did not understand;

How blood and sweat seeped through sand,

and made the refugee problem yesterday,

that of bodies and charities for today.

5

They are so hard;

Those names.

Deir Yassine.

Tel Zaatar.

Karameh.

They are so hard.

Hard as hearts that made them.

They are so hard.

Those names.

For they have died long ago –

Those names.

Hard.

6

Tonight, my sister called me.

Beirut is calm now and she

is storytelling and saying sorry.

Sorry she had cried last night.

It was a car bomb; the blood

had covered her and her friend

had moaned. She saw twenty

seven deaths. And she cried

across the water and down

the country lane where I lived.

Tonight my sister called me,

To say sorry she had cried last night.

We laughed and joked and said, see

We can survive: tomorrow she'll phone to

                      say sorry we laughed tonight.

7

Phew-oot it exploded and showered

Paper upon paper within the cage.

People rushed out and picked a few.

Pooh-poohing they laughed and jeered.

Pointing that way the enemy Defence:

Please take that road out of your cage.

Perhaps the Eastern sector will open.

Probably, said a few and everyone nodded.

Pitta bread is available, shouted someone.

Pale laughing faces lined up and

Papers all red floated nowhere.

We will eat now

and escape tonight

To death some bow

others stand and fight.

and Pitta bread was sold tonight.

8

"*Never again!*" said the Jew.

Never again: shackled animals:

Packed and killed: six million

Kills. Never again.

Never again the ghetto for me.

Never again the laughter and the jeer.

Never again the number tattooed.

Teeth pulled out; live skeletons burnt.

Never never never again.

For now a State I have, a home,

A land; and never again will I die.

"*Never again*" burnt into my people's

National conscience. Never again say I.

Never again say we all loudly loudly loudly.

And the echo is heard all across the land.

But the world will not listen to the new Jew.

It never listened to the old.

"*Never again*" will have to wait

Palestinians all.

For it has been and will be

again again again and again,

Palestinians all.

Betrayed and despised all.

And then…

"*Never again!*" said the nouveou Jew.

9

The Rats

To J. E. Hegarty

Lebanese ladies bejewelled and lovely

Sat 'Chez Emile' for fresh fish and

Oriental delicacies. A night most

European and more.

Dazzling were they and their entourage:

Ministers from London New York

and Kiev. They laughed and lolled.

Unmoved.

The war is over, and the liberators

Beat. Time. Time. Time. to the. Thud.

Thud. Thudding of not so distant bombs.

Hidden by smoke people scurry

in silence, rat-like, soon to become

rat food; replete and fat.

Ladies, the meat you eat is bloodied.

It is not Kosher.

The rats eat hallowéd meat.

Its blood was spilled and its late

tenant to a new Jerusalem sped.

Ladies. Ladies.

10

Let's joke about it.

It is funny you know.

They are sweet and childlike

and so

survive.

Let's joke about it.

The government is now resigned.

Premier and Tourism made redundant:

and so

survive.

Come. Let's joke about it.

In laughing we pull back the tears.

There is death enough without reflections

on bubbled cheeks.

And when the tears roll: and the bubbles blow:

cover your face,

and feel it like a man.

Let's joke about it.

11

Did you realize,   Seen with your own eyes

That it is over now,   This is the final bow?

Did you foresee,   That you I and we

One day will forget,   Ahead our vision set?

Did you dream,   Of loves that seem

And loves that are not   Dead all forgot?

Did you?

Did you?

We did not.

My simple-minded rhyme,

Will remind you in time.

And for every reason:

Snatched out of season.

Did you foresee?

12

A Palestinian once met a Jew

and asked, "*How do you live my friend*?"

"*In toil,*" the other replied. "*In toil*

and in freedom. My friend. I have

a house. Large and white. A garden

from a desert grown and children

for future toil.

My children explore their new home

and everyday find a new toy.

A doll – old and ragged. A wooden horse

chipped and loved…"

"*A wooden horse, my friend? In a*

white cupboard and spots on it? A

mane so proud?

Why my friend,

it was mine a long time ago.

Mine, my friend."

13

The four horses of the Apocalypse

Rode in triumph over stone and flesh.

Forward they surged and took all before 'em.

The four horses of the Apocalypse.

And a tiny fifth came behind

Trotting merrily

Spelling treachery.

And it grew – the fifth horse of the

Apocalypse.

14

The battle is over.

The dead most relieved.

15

To my daughter Catherine

We will build a memorial.

We will build statues.

Name after name will be inscribed

Celebrating the glory of the fallen.

Unwilling martyrs;

Their eternal flame snuffed out for good.

We will remember them one by one,

As we play our daily lives.

We will remember and we will build –

What was it we will build?

16

Interlude the First

"*That is my water!*" said the fox

upstream from the sheep.

"*No, mine!*" echoed the sheep.

"*I have drunk it for years before*

you came."

And the eagle, proud and sage, replied

"*It is my little sphere. I will piss*

in it at the source and claim it

my people's."

The fox smiled and drank.

The sheep thirsted and died.

The eagle flew high amongst the stars:

its wings striped against the dark sky.

17

Black smoke.

So black I could see nothing.

Black souls.

So black they could see nothing.

White eyes.

So white they could see nothing.

White souls.

So white they could not be seen.

18

If he could cheat death

For Palestine – he would.

But he couldn't do it,

and so died.

19

The martyred list:

Abu Muhammad proud and tall.

Ali, Jaber, and Mustapha

and his brothers strong men all.

George, Antoine of Christian faith

Shirin, Nabila, and Leila

and others – thousands upon thousands,

Cheated all.

They all live

The martyred list.

Live to see more.

Cheated all.

20

The Numbers Game

The Red Cross says twenty thousand died.

They say less – perhaps one thousand died.

Numbers vary according to those who died.

And they will always play the numbers game.

That's their tragedy.

Yours, my friend, is the first that

died.

One.

One.

21

"Mother"

To Dr. Amal Shamaa

"*We'll make it,*" she said with a quiet smile.

Eyes reddened she looked at us and smiled again.

Soft familiar voices reassured one another:

"*We're all in the same – what do I mean? –*

Well, the same, you know. We are all".

Outside, truthfully, it was red fiery Hell.

Shell upon shell each fell as all was black.

Dust, stones, glass, and a little wood.

We heard voices: loud frightened and gurgling.

One man cried, "*mother!*" head resting on arms

and one leg crossed. The other leg was

now dust and clouds. He nodded at us.

And cried "*mother!*" by way of greeting.

"*Is it not strange,*" we wondered, "*how*

strong men and old men cry "mother!"

When they've lost a leg? Is it not strange?"

We said. The reply came from a baby.

It lay kicking covered red and jellied in blood.

"It's from its mother. That's its mother's

blood. The baby's fine". He smiled at us.

"Where's its mother?" – and he smiled

by way of apology and pointed to an

empty stretcher. The baby kicked.

A boy was bumped in and its clothes cut.

"Didn't I tell you not to bring dead ones in

here! Didn't I! didn't I!"

"How do I know they're dead. I only drive."

"Can't we use his blood?

Can't we use his blood?"

Screamed an old – old – woman.

"Mother. Mother. Sit and wait. You son

needs no blood now. Not now. Mother."

She sat. She nodded at us absently.

We tried to fight the horror.

They are only cuts really.

Look hard at them and grit your teeth.

We're all in the same.

"We'll probably all die as long as it

don't hurt".

A nurse cried.

She said she hated Israeli men.

She told us how the shelling went

and the noise

"tin tin tin tin tin tin tin…"

Someone behind her smiled.

Embarrassed.

We listened and watched.

Some walked and sidestepped pools of blood.

"We'll make it," she said with a quiet smile.

"We'll make it".

We nodded without belief.

And in my heart I poured her woes.

We'll make it.

Oh how I wished I were there

To hold her

and say

"*Now I know why old men cry 'mother!'*".

Oh how I wished I were there

as I watched Lebanon burnt

and West Beirut burning,

Burning,

not knowing when burnt –

instead of seeing it all on celluloid.

"*We'll make it – we will –*

my love; sister;

Mother!"

22

I stand ready to die

for homeland and dreams.

When I die, they will put

a picture up on falling walls.

Martyred for the homeland

Martyred for freedom's sake.

And when someone asks who

what where how old I was,

No one will know.

I will. My age but one second.

The time to die.

For what comes after is nothing –

and what was before even less.

23

When we are finished

And all war is but an echo,

When the earth is cool again

And rats fear us for cleanliness,

When we can think again

And maybe laugh at all this,

When we have mourned forty days

And white scarved women wail no more,

When we can see in clear light

And breathe a cleaner air,

When oh when – all this we can

And more besides: then we will be.

But until then my love my mother my land

I will sit here dreaming and looking: gun in hand.

24

My land is like a lovely tree.

It bears fruit and is green.

It shadows me when I am in need

And warms me with its heat.

If feeds me in hunger

And waters my family.

But when I go I forget our lovely

Tree

and all it gives.

Vague dreams and memories

serve my nightly daydreams –

but as to form shape and feel

I have to see to believe.

My land is like a lovely tree.

25

The guns are silent now.

Fathers search for their sons.

It is a strange world, where

father buries son,

mourns him,

and comforts his mother.

He died for the homeland, mother.

The homeland.

The son's mother looks up

far far away

and sees her son's future

happy prosperous and devoted.

Homeless, sonless, and brainless

she repeats.

He died for the homeland, father.

That he did.

Palestine Pound Notes found amongst the poet's late father's papers.

A Return: The Siege of Beirut

Book Two: The Living

1

The Little Feast

"The little Feast is now here;

A fattened calf or two:

And if a calf there is not:

Well! Well! Let's slaughter a blond girl instead

For the Little Feast is now here".

Thus sang little children

all decked in blue and red.

Hair in pretty bunches black and long.

Sugared almonds and shining coins.

A rickety fair with swings and candy

floss; like red red hair.

The children sing: eyes wide and staring.

These are happy times

and the little children sing for them.

Their parents

move

    and smile

       and pretend.

For the Little Feast is now here

and all is quiet in West Beirut.

2

In a cavern as black as death,

There are no echoes left to feel.

All is quiet now: and the politician

has the field.

We will not stand aside and wait forever

and we – we will stall and stall.

Let us all negotiate with one voice.

Other options remain.

Meanwhile we will burn the rubbish

and eat the smuggled food.

Bury our dead

and unearth our lost ones.

Pray for peace

and talk of war.

Our children will remember all this:

for they are limbless, eyeless , and alone.

And we – their parents:

We hold their hands

See for their future

Comfort their solitude –

They are soul-less too.

We – we hear the echoes reverberate

on the hollow corpse that is become our home.

3

To the victims

Beirut burns tonight.

How come when all is quiet in West Beirut?

Beirut will burn tomorrow.

Why when they negotiate?

Beirut was burnt

    is burning,

    and will always burn.

No. for they have no victors and no vanquished

written into their very soul.

Beirut burns tonight.

Its ashes are minute particles

Charred in Arab faith.

Blackened in brotherhood.

Bitter smelling in false expectation.

And floating to oblivion in treachery

yet to come.

That is why Beirut burns tonight.

4

Let me tell you how your father died.

The same as did your brothers.

Less cruelly than did your sisters.

I lived, for you were within me.

Let me tell you how your father died.

Not so distant from where your brothers did.

Not so near to how your sisters went.

I lived, for you were in need of me.

And now that you are grown

No longer a child but a full grown boy.

Go – Go out and fight with bitterness,

Find out why a father, brother, and sister-less.

My son

My little one.

Your father died an innocent hero –

Felled; as you no doubt will too.

5

To Anne Blakeman

Now I am dead *"think only this of me"*:

Not that I died a hero for my land.

Not that there is a fresh and green land

Somewhere in foreign cities Palestine called.

Less that I fell fighting treachery.

Now I am dead *"think only this of me"*:

Not that I loved my home.

Not that I lived for home –

Somewhere in a foreign clime not of Palestine.

Less that I died shielding my brethren.

Now I am dead *"think only this of me"*:

That I died friendless, homeless, nationless.

That I died hated, forgotten, perjured.

That I died without prayers for Palestine.

That I died in bitterness and in blood.

Now I am dead *"think only this of me"*:

That in some foreign land I forgot be.

Now I am dead:

        think not anything:

                of me.

6

Interlude the Second

The Wild West Barn Dance

Now! Take your partner by the hand.

Shake it hard and turn him round.

Throw him up and clap your hands.

Tap your knees and cross your arms.

One more time: do it again: twirl him round.

Now! Push your partner once or twice.

Take your gun and flick it too.

Take your aim and twist your face.

Raise your brow and fire away.

One more time: do it again: watch him fall.

Now! Take your bow and blow your gun.

Laugh at him and shoot again.

Rape his wife and kiss his gals.

Share them round and turn them o'er.

One more time: do it again: wipe the blood.

Now! Tell your lies and wait away.

The cavalry'll come and clap their hands.

Cowboy Ron and his posse too.

Smile at him and look all sweet.

One more time: do it again: count the dead.

7

People wait and watch.

All in a row.

Leaving nothing behind.

Every memory a secret door.

Some are dead others not much.

To them that are;

In a day or two:

None remain,

Except the death: leveller of all.

But to them that are not;

Ere long will be.

Towards a tomorrow: hope:

Redemption: and ease.

All for loss of nothing.

Yet all for all.

Especially those too young:

Doomed to early age.

8

Ruins

To S. E. Mikdadi

In Sidon Tyre and around,

Speak Roman ruins of beauty unmatched.

Here, an amphitheatre silenced ages gone by;

But once shaking and echoing to the very skies

With one hundred thousand joyless voices.

Pillars, sarcophagi, mosaics, and delicate idols,

All line by line to gaze at and ponder.

Every ruin speaks for itself;

Of Roman love, war, and death:

Amidst bustling life.

Of Alexander's siege, and:

Ten thousand to the sword he once put.

Of a Roman wedding,

Wrestling, chariots racing, gladiators –

Christian and Jew.

For in Sidon Tyre and around:

Every ruin speaks for itself.

And today little is seen and less is heard.

There are new ruins now.

Where, when, why and how;

Are questions often with Romans met.

Not today; with dust afloat; blood all wet.

In a thousand years, or so, a guide:

These are Roman ruins that stand here;

These were Arab ruins maybe there.

Such sarcophagi where Rome her dead did lay;

Such grassy field where Lebanon hers did, they say.

Buy your book of ancient Rome in her day:

Of Lebanon, all in all, it was by the way.

9

Good night gentlemen, one and all.

Good night ladies, one and all.

This war we present to-night,

Is like a lover in sleepless plight.

He conjures a spirit most powerfully,

Dreams of joys yet to come.

And for very dream his passion spent.

His partner, confused, retreats anew.

Semblance, hypocrisy, unnecessary pain.

If honest toil were his wakeful dream.

Then their sleeplessness love covered would seem.

This war we present tonight

Is not only like but more: futile.

In the lover it is as it would seem;

In our war it seems as if it is.

Good night.

Good night.

10

To Mr. President

Palestine.

Say it backward or

Anagrammatise:

It.

Is.

Pale.

Sale.

Let.

Tip.

Pit.

In.

Line.

    Tale.

    Tail.

    Ail.

    Ale.

Nail.

Pile.

Tile.

Sit.

Sip.

Lip.

And more.

Many more.

A hundred, perhaps,

A thousand.

A wordgame.

A game in words.

A house of cards.

Palestine.

A master at the game.

Our American pals play it so well.

This game in words.

Al Nakba 1948 or Palestinians fleeing Gaza 1967 – variously attributed to either occasion, photographer unknown.

A Return: The Siege of Beirut

Book Three: The Dead

The Dead

To my sister Lina

1

To be born in 1947 was an act of faith.

White-scarved women – so they say – attended the birth.

Behind, murmured many a man in that erstwhile

faith. A state was born. Displaced diaspora:

At last a national home and grand family lore.

Stillborn the state of Palestine: diaspora new.

The world at large approved, and shut one eye.

An infant cried lustily, and they smiled

When, conscienceless and consciousless, he nothing saw.

So, at least, my teacher said to me. It is

Difficult, I think, to part pictures built

In memory, from stories my teacher said to me.

But what, what went wrong? I asked in an

Innocence that had not lived before.

My teacher, the collective conscience of my people,

Explained all. He shouted, bantered and

Talked at me all the while waving his hands.

I understood nothing, was not meant to understand.

What I tell, imaged its form through my mind.

Of people lost, found, and lost again.

True to fact or not: It is, in truth, human emotions.

Let me, then, cast that mind far far behind.

2

In the beginning was the people.

Holy land behind and exile before.

Marching, dragging forward surge, towards a future.

Future unknown from whence born exiled souls.

Temporary camps for years to come, some

Never to return – others connecting endless

Day to endless day with hope.

Thus days fused into nights the daylong time.

And still – no return.

3

Resolved: some left the camps.

Only you – and you alone – will regain the loss.

But many a man, woman, and child –

Beware the hypocritical phrase –

Even they, stayed, unchanging except to the left.

Damned by truth, history, and the camp.

People multiplied at the speed of words.

Then there were too many words:

Euphoric. That was all.

July twenty-third.

Suez came and went.

People, words, and confusion pyramid upwards:

Get blown and come back again.

4

I well remember how to Nablus my father and I.

Never betray your trust; I shall give to you now.

Look: there! My father's land. Here the square.

Over there fields: plentiful food.

Very apt in moderate climes. Clothes colourful.

Every one embroidered by land-licked hands.

We had tea – black and sweet and strong.

In a roofless shack with Fatima and folk.

I stared at her face. Tattooed: she laughed.

I well remember how final it all was.

That temporary camp. Soon to return.

5

One day we tried and lost.

And on the seventh day we awoke.

Two exiles were never to be the same again:

Camps will temporise.

Palestinians everywhere will silence that word.

Jerusalem, Karameh and Amman.

Beirut, Tal Zaatar and bloodied soil.

6

It was said of Lebanon once –

Many things were said:

No victor no vanquished.

General consensus: all shared alike.

Fine balances reliant on fine spirits.

And many more.

Freedom of the exile.

Love of the free.

Even, business as usual.

Palestine's last stand.

That it was wrong – crying wrong –

That it was sad – damning sad –

That it was tragic – killing tragic –

It *was* Palestine's last stand:

Against faceless metal, swooping metal;

Exploding metal.

All patience was lost – being lost:

Menachem, shalom! said the leader of the free world.

Mr. President: we never hurt that baby.

They burnt her – or was it him?

Mr. President: those we killed weren't on that picture.

Mr. President – of the free world.

7

Row upon row of Palestine's last stand;

Dispersed once again to friendly nations.

Oh, how silent this friendship was.

Silent as the dead.

And Jordan for the Jordanians.

Syria for the Syrians,

And Lebanon for the Lebanese.

Reconciled, forgetful, and forgotten.

The dead always are – unless they talk.

Mr. President will not have it so.

8

In the beginning was the People.

And the people asked for justice, and the

People was without home and void; and

darkness was upon the face of the exile.

And the Spirit of the People moved upon

the face of the homeland.

And the People said, Let there be

justice. And the People thought

it was good.

9

In the end was the Dead.

And the Dead spoke not for it had learnt.

And the Dead left for a new exile.

Taking the dying with it.

And the Dead asked for justice.

And was told it had died in vain. And

the Dead answered not for it had learnt.

Learnt that a man without a home:

      a man without name:

      a man without family:

the exiled: without Palestine

is dead. And the Dead cannot be killed.

10

This – so short and never written –

My teacher never said to me.

Diaspora new: stillborn the state of Palestine.

My heart bleeds for you:

Your voice, your words, your very hand.

I understand your very smile.

Your very death.

And in the beginning was the word:

And the word was Palestine.

Cast the new mind far far ahead.

To Palestine. Yes.

To Palestine. Yes.

Painted into a Corner   Faysal Mikdadi

Printed in Great Britain
by Amazon